CASE STUDY RESEARCH

A Program Evaluation Guide for Librarians

Ravonne A. Green

 LIBRARIES UNLIMITED

AN IMPRINT OF ABC-CLIO, LLC

Santa Barbara, California • Denver, Colorado • Oxford, England

Library of Congress Cataloging-in-Publication Data

Green, Ravonne A.
   Case study research : a program evaluation guide for librarians / Ravonne A. Green.
      p. cm.
   Includes bibliographical references and index.
   ISBN 978–1–59158–860–3 (pbk.) — ISBN 978–1–59158–861–0 (ebook)   1. Libraries—Evaluation.
2. Public services (Libraries)—Evaluation. 3. Information literacy—Study and teaching—Evaluation—
Case studies. 4. Evaluation. 5. Case method. 6. Research—Methodology. I. Title.
   Z678.85.G74   2011
   027.0072—dc23   2011029211

ISBN: 978–1–59158–860–3
EISBN: 978–1–59158–861–0

15 14 13 12 11   1 2 3 4 5

This book is also available on the World Wide Web as an eBook.
Visit www.abc-clio.com for details.

Libraries Unlimited
An Imprint of ABC-CLIO, LLC

ABC-CLIO, LLC
130 Cremona Drive, P.O. Box 1911
Santa Barbara, California 93116-1911

This book is printed on acid-free paper ∞

Manufactured in the United States of America

Contents

Introduction

Charles and Mertler (2004) identify three purposes of case study research: to provide vivid descriptions of an individual or phenomenon; to provide explanations; and to provide evaluation data. Case study research can identify strengths and weaknesses that may lead to modifications and improvements.

Dudden (2007) identified five core methods—needs assessment, quality improvement, benchmarking, library performance standards, and outcomes measurement—that should mark effective library program evaluation. Case studies using a systems approach incorporate all of these methods to provide a holistic view of one program or segment of an organization. The case study is part of the big picture. The researcher looks holistically at the setting to understand linkages among systems (Marshall & Rossman, 1995). Stake (1995) defined a case as a bounded system. Using the system metaphor, cases are envisioned as holistic entities with individual parts that function in their system or environment. *The Guiding Principles for Evaluators* (American Evaluation Association, 2004) include systematic inquiry as one of their five guiding principles.

Operating within the system metaphor, the researcher works with the stakeholders within an organization to gain a clear picture of how the program is a part of the overall network of planning, instruction, and assessment. The entire assessment team works to provide a rich description of the program and its contributions to the organization or system.

This book is intended to offer readers an introduction to case study research in relation to a program-related process for a fictional South Central case. Focus questions are provided at the beginning of each chapter to help the reader concentrate on key topics and terms. Chapters include end sections outlining major program evaluation theories and concepts, and the Joint Committee on Standards for Educational Evaluation (1994). Other features include case study applications and exercises at the end of each chapter.

Chapter 1 provides a general introduction to case studies as a form of program evaluation. This chapter includes background information for someone who is new to the practice of program evaluation as well as the purposes and roles that evaluators assume while conducting a program case study. Chapter 1 also includes a section of advantages, disadvantages, and themes and a glossary of case study terms.

A simulated case study is presented in Chapter 2. This case has numerous flaws. The reader will detect the flaws and perfect this case through reading the text and completing end-of-chapter case exercises. A Case Application is provided at the end of each section with application comments for the South Central case. These perceptions by the evaluator should provide discussion topics and comments. The chapter exercises are intended as group activities to simulate an actual work environment. This text advocates a multiple-methods approach to validate case study results.

For the simulated case, the experience demonstrates that of an external consultant. However, the multiple-method case study analysis may be used by a campus committee if this is the most appropriate or financially feasible means for accomplishing a real-life assessment.

Case study research analysis involves developing and using skills in evaluating the proposal. These are discussed in Chapter 3. Bounding the case and analyzing the context is covered in Chapter 5. Chapter 6 explains planning questions and criteria. Readers will learn about identifying design and data collection methods in Chapter 7, while Chapter 8 discusses establishing and maintaining appropriate political, ethical, and interpersonal relationships. Chapter 9 covers collecting, analyzing, and interpreting quantitative and qualitative data. Reporting the case study is the topic of Chapter 10. The text deals with all of these issues and guides the reader through the process of using case study matrices and selecting appropriate qualitative software. Chapter 11 describes data analysis software.

REFERENCES

American Evaluation Association. *Guiding Principles for Evaluators*. Fairhaven, MA: American Evaluation Association, 2004. http://www.eval.org/Publications/GuidingPrinciples.asp.

Charles, C., & Mertler, C. *Introduction to Educational Research*. Boston: Allyn & Bacon, 2004.

Dudden, R. *Using Benchmarking, Needs Assessment, Quality Improvement, Outcome Measurement, and Library Standards*. Medical Library Association Guides. New York: Neal-Schuman, 2007.

Joint Committee on Standards for Educational Evaluation. *The Program Evaluation Standards*, 2nd ed. Thousand Oaks, CA: Corwin Pr., 1994.

Marshall, C., & Rossman, G. *Designing Qualitative Research*, 2nd ed. Thousand Oaks, CA: Sage, 1995.

Stake, R. *The Art of Case Study Research*. Thousand Oaks, CA: Sage, 1995.

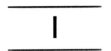

I

Purposes, Uses, and Conceptual Distinctions of Case Studies

FOCUS QUESTIONS

Why would you choose to use the case study method for evaluation purposes?
Will your case be particularistic, descriptive, heuristic, or a multi-case study?
Why do you think the case study method will yield a thicker (more complete) description for your
    study than another method that you could use?

MAJOR THEORIES AND CONCEPTS

- Case study research seeks to identify behavioral and procedural patterns in a naturalistic
  setting.
- Case study research provides an intensive, holistic description and analysis of a single instance,
  phenomenon, or social unit.
- Case study research may be empirical in nature but will have rich, deep descriptions of data.
- Case studies are particularistic, descriptive, and heuristic, or multi-methods.
- Collective case studies are used in performing a program evaluation to provide an accurate or
  holistic program of the entire organization or program or to provide peer evaluations.

Dudden (2007) identified five core methods (needs assessment, quality improvement,
benchmarking, library performance standards, and outcomes measurement) that should
mark effective library program evaluation. Case studies using a systems approach
incorporate all of these methods to provide a holistic view of one program or segment
of an organization. The case study is part of the big picture; the researcher looks holistically at the setting to understand linkages among systems (Marshall & Rossman,
1995). Stake (1995) defined a case as a bounded system. Using the system metaphor,
cases are envisioned as holistic entities with individual parts that function in their system or environment. The Guiding Principles for Evaluators (American Evaluation
Association, 2004) include systematic inquiry as one of their five guiding principles.
    Operating in the system metaphor, the researcher works with the stakeholders within
an organization to gain a clear picture of how the program is a part of the overall network

of planning, instruction, and assessment. The entire assessment team works to provide a rich description of the program and its contributions to the organization or system.

CASE STUDY: DEFINITIONS

Yin (1981) defines a case study as an empirical inquiry that investigates a contemporary phenomenon in depth, within its real-life context, and relies on multiple sources of evidence, with data needing to converge in a triangulating fashion (p. 28). Yin's definition covers the logic of design, data collection techniques, and specific approaches to data analysis. Yin's focus is on the research process.

Stake (1995) defines the case in terms of the unit of study and focuses on bounding the case. Merriam (1998) and Wolcott (1992) seek a more holistic definition of the qualitative case study. Merriam (1998) defines a case study as an "intensive, holistic description and analysis of a single instance, phenomenon, or social unit" (p. 27). Creswell (2007) notes that case studies are not just a form of qualitative research. Case studies usually incorporate a mixed methodology that includes quantitative elements and qualitative methods such as interviews, surveys, and focus groups.

Quantitative research provides numerical data in the form of survey responses, gate counts, circulation or reference statistics, and benchmarking ratios. Quantitative techniques are helpful for providing basic information but often fall short of explaining a problem or illustrating outcomes.

Qualitative data such as interviews and focus groups often give us a more in-depth picture of a problem or program but can sometimes be slanted or lack clarity. Case study data have the advantage of combining both techniques and providing a clear, unbiased picture of the entire case, phenomenon, problem, or program.

Programs or systems may be defined as the unit that is to be assessed within the boundary of a larger unit. For example, if we are to assess a library program such as an information literacy program, the information literacy program is part of the library system and the university system. It is part of a larger network of libraries and library policies. For example, the individuals who developed the information literacy program probably referred to the Association of College and Research Library Information Literacy Principles and to the information literacy programs of benchmarking institutions.

Bounding a case within a system provides us with the proper context. The larger system provides the policies, procedures, budget, personnel, and standards for the program. Identifying and understanding the system(s) within which the case is bounded is the first essential element of program assessment. If we are planning to assess an information literacy program at a Research I institution, it would not be appropriate or within the bounds of the case to compare that program to the information literacy program at a small, technical college.

Stake (1995) insists that the absolute essential elements of a case study are the definition of the case, the list of research questions, identification of research assistants or participants, data sources, allocation of time, expenses, and intended reporting strategies and timelines. Creswell (1998) adds to this list the context of the case and analysis techniques such as holistic analysis, embedded analysis, and within-case and cross-case analysis.

THE PURPOSE OF CASE STUDY RESEARCH

Case studies help us to understand processes such as describing the context and discovering explanations for a problem that is being studied. "Case studies help us to understand processes of events, projects, and programs and to discover context characteristics that will shed light on an issue or object" (Sanders, 1981, p. 44).

Stake (1981) argues that case study research is more concrete because it resonates with experience and is rooted within the context. This knowledge is distinguishable from the abstract, formal knowledge derived from other research designs. Case study knowledge is more developed by reader interpretation as readers bring to a case their own experience and understanding, which lead to generalizations when new data for the case are added to old data. Unlike traditional research, the reader participates in extending generalizations to reference populations (Stake, 1981, pp. 35–36).

Charles and Mertler (2004) identify three purposes of case study research. The first is to provide vivid descriptions of an individual or phenomenon. For example, library researchers may wish to provide outcomes data to demonstrate the effectiveness of an information literacy program. They may have administered pretests and posttests and perhaps collected surveys or questionnaires. These quantitative methods may demonstrate that there has been a difference in skills or knowledge. However, there may be discrepancies in the data or questions or concerns about the responses to certain items. Surveys and other quantitative methods generally raise more questions to answer with more data.

Another researcher might design a case study to answer these questions. This researcher may select six seniors who took Information Literacy 101 at the beginning of their first year of college and have attended a series of these courses each year for the last four years. The results of this study would be compared to the results among students who are enrolled in the same major. The researcher could also select seniors from six different majors and compare results across the curriculum. The researcher may decide to have two separate groups and to compare the results from both groups.

Cronbach (1980) and Patton (2002) concur that case studies have a distinctive place in evaluation research. They mention four case study applications in the area of program evaluation. Perhaps the most important function of a case study in program evaluation is to explain or to answer the "why" and "how" questions (Yin, 2009).

A second purpose for case study research is to provide explanations. Often quantitative research raises "why" questions. It is not sufficient to know that the circulation count has been down. Case study research seeks to identify behavioral and procedural patterns. A researcher might notice that the circulation count is down 85 percent in the English literature section, accounting for the majority of the overall decrease in circulation. The researcher decides to distribute a survey to the English department, which indicates that the entire current English faculty is well satisfied with library services, library instruction, and the materials that are available in the library. The researcher then decides to conduct a focus group to involve students currently enrolled in English courses.

One of the students in the focus group comments that she only checks out books when she has to and that she prefers to use online databases. The researcher thinks that perhaps some new databases might have been added in the library that students are using instead of checking out books. He interviews the reference librarians and they tell him that nothing new has been added in the last year. Actually, the library has had to cancel one database that the English department had used heavily because of budget cuts.

The researcher sets up interviews with a sample group of faculty and students who have taught or have been enrolled in English literature courses within the past year.

The interviews kept pointing to one interesting fact: Mr. Smith, who had taught English literature for the past twenty years at ABC University, required his students to check out ten books each during the second week of class for their term papers. Mr. Smith retired last spring and his successor did not require term papers. Therefore, that the new English literature professor does not require term papers is probably related to the decrease in the English literature circulation count.

The researcher may then look at all of the information that he or she has gathered to form a case. The researcher may use other methods to confirm or disconfirm the theory about the drop in the circulation count being related to Mr. Smith's retirement. This case study should point out relational patterns. Relational patterns indicate that two or more events or traits appear to be related.

Explanations sometimes point out causal patterns, which are patterns that a researcher would note as having either a negative or positive effect on a particular phenomenon. We typically think of causal patterns as negative influences, but causal patterns can also be positive influences. Professors may offer their students extra credit for reading African American novels in an African American literature course. This requirement would have a positive effect on the circulation count in this area.

The researcher definitely wants to identify causal factors and report these. For example, if a shifting project is occurring and the English literature section has been moved to another floor and there are no directional signs, patrons may be extremely frustrated if they have come to the library to check out English literature books and cannot find them. Students may not be checking out books in this section because they are having difficulty locating them. Both surveys and experimental designs fall short of explaining their phenomenon.

Surveys provide us with raw data. We know how many people agree or disagree with a statement but we do not know why people agree or disagree. We know that people are satisfied or dissatisfied but we do not know why. Neither do we know how to improve our performance from the raw data that we have from surveys.

Experimental designs give us comparison data. We can look at pretest and posttest results and assume that a treatment was successful, but without narrative data, we do not know if the treatment was successful or if something else contributed to the difference in pretest and posttest scores. For example, an English professor may have been teaching information literacy skills to a group of students before they took the library information literacy course. These students may do extremely well on a pretest in the library information literacy course, and there may be little difference in the posttest results. A library information literacy class that had not had any prior information literacy instruction may not do so well on the pretest. Individual test scores could also vary depending on a student's high school background in this area.

Case studies serve to describe, illustrate, and enlighten the researcher about issues and questions that may arise from quantitative data or less descriptive qualitative methods. For example, your library may have conducted a survey indicating that 50 percent of the students on your campus have never used the library—quantitative data. You may be considering a study to discover how, accurately, to determine the reasons that students are not using the library. If I am to ask, "Why are 50 percent of the students not using the library?" I can construct a case study using quantitative data, interviews, focus groups, and other methods to try to find answers to these questions, and the report would become a case study. I can take my case a step further and perform a similar study at another institution or perhaps several benchmarking institutions. My case study then becomes a multiple or comparative case study. I can do cross-case analyses, further strengthening the reliability, validity, and generalizability of my research. We will discuss these concepts in more detail in later chapters.

The third purpose of case study research is to provide evaluation data. Case study research is useful for evaluating programs, individuals, and settings. The data that may be derived from a case study will help to paint the whole picture. For example, a rubric that is used for an individual employee evaluation will show a list of competencies and deficiencies. However, if a supervisor has kept absentee records, email, and other correspondence from one employee and from other employees in that department and has interviewed the employee regarding the evaluation, the supervisor can form a case that is much more complete than one formed with a simple metric such as a rubric.

Case study research can identify program strengths and weaknesses and may lead to modifications and improvements. A strengths, weaknesses, opportunities, and threats (SWOT) analysis may identify general areas of strength and weakness. A case study researcher can then analyze these areas more thoroughly by interviewing individuals or conducting an in-depth evaluation.

The case study approach is an excellent qualitative research method when factors and relationships may be directly observed. Case study researchers attempt to gather in-depth material related to an individual or to a program or event. Powell and Connaway (2004) suggest a case study for an investigation of staff burnout in a reference department. If a librarian had a research question about staff burnout, case study data would be corroborated with questionnaires, interviews, observation, and document analysis. For example, why does there seem to be such a high turnover in the reference department?

Librarians in that department have made several comments about staff burnout but no one has given specific reasons for burnout. The problem could be one supervisor who has difficulty getting along with people; these employees may have felt intimidated about expressing their issues on a survey form if that difficult supervisor would be reading the results of the survey. However, this information might come out in individual interviews with an outside consultant.

Several issues may be revealed in an interview. For example, there may be two employees in that department suffering from terminal illnesses who have to be absent, frequently causing other people in that department to work extra hours. The other employees may not mention this reason on a survey because they would not want to jeopardize the other employees' jobs.

The causes could be environmental. For example, the central heating and air (CHA) system in the reference section may not work properly. Employees may have stopped listing this because they have been told that funds are not available to purchase a new CHA unit. An outside researcher would only need to observe for a few minutes on an extremely hot or cold day to see why employees could not stand to work in an environment that is 40 degrees in the winter or 100 degrees in the summer.

Case studies are particularly effective for longitudinal studies and for studies with a lot of complex issues. Longitudinal studies can show an effective progression of data in many areas such as collection development, circulation, reference, and technical services. Many library studies have layers of issues that need a more thorough treatment than just a quick survey.

CASE STUDY ADVANTAGES

Some additional advantages of using the case study method in program evaluation include triangulating data using multiple methods and providing data that are rich with examples and stories. The case study method captures what is important to the participants and may provide outcomes information that had not been relayed using quantitative methods (Russ-Eft & Preskill, 2001, p. 174).

CASE STUDY DISADVANTAGES

Some of the disadvantages to using the case study design might include a lack of generalizability and evaluator bias. Case studies are not always time and cost effective (Russ-Eft & Preskill, 2001, p. 174).

CASE STUDY THEMES

Case study themes are typically naturalistic generalizations and may either be particularistic, descriptive, heuristic, or collective. The first, particularistic case studies, focus on a particular individual or problem and may be referred to as intrinsic case studies (Stake, 1995). The researcher has an interest in the case. Particularistic case studies deal with understanding or interpreting an individual's behavior or attitude. The main characteristic of a particularistic case is that this type of case can examine a specific instance and yet illuminate a general problem (Olson in Hoaglin et al., 1982, pp. 138–139). Since particularistic case studies focus on an individual or an individual problem or program, the researcher will include extensive descriptions of the individual who is the focus of the case study.

Particularistic case studies are thick (complete) with character analysis. Character analysis does not just involve telling a story about this individual but is getting at the root of what has caused this person to react in a certain manner. The researcher looks for consistencies and inconsistencies. The researcher might, for example, notice that the individual who is being studied reacts one way to one individual and in another way toward someone else in a similar circumstance. If this individual is a library director, the library director may appear to be extremely accommodating toward administrators but act in a condescending manner toward subordinates. A circulation librarian may permit an administrator to check out a stack of books without producing a library card even though a sign by the circulation desk states that all patrons must have a library card to check out books. This same librarian may deny first-year college students the privilege to check out books when they cannot produce a library card. The focus throughout the case study is clearly on the individual. The researcher attempts to give credence to the individual as the seat of the problem by presenting as many conflict situations as possible where the individual reacts in a negative fashion.

Particularistic studies generally occur over time to give the researcher the opportunity to adequately and accurately observe an individual's behavior. Particularistic case studies are typically only useful in dealing with one person; however, they can sometimes be generalized to similar character types. We have all had the experience of reading a case study that was written about a library employee in a distant location and exclaiming, "I know this person!" In fact, we generally do not know this person but know someone who has character traits that are amazingly similar.

Particularistic studies typically do not deal with just one isolated incident. Sometimes employees can point back to one incident that was the catalyst for a negative chain of events. However, this one incident is indicative of this person's general behavior and attitudes. An interviewee might make a comment such as, "That was when he showed his true colors!" Such comments let the case study researcher know that the incident that the interviewee has just reported was the beginning of the awareness of the problem with this individual. Denzin (1989) refers to such a moment as "the major epiphany" (p. 129).

"Cumulative epiphanies" occur when an individual overreacts to a situation based on pent-up stresses (Denzin, 1989, p. 129). For example, Sue may report to her supervisor that "all she did was say, 'good morning' to Jack and he bit my head off." As a researcher, you might mention this incident to Jack. Jack might inform you that he was very angry with Sue on that morning because she was scheduled to help him with two bibliographic instruction sessions at 8:00 a.m. and 9:00 a.m. She had not shown up for either one of them and he had been left to manage the reference desk alone and had not had a break all morning. Sue had done this to him repeatedly over the last year. He had reported her behavior to his supervisor and she had done nothing. She always defended Sue. When Sue finally arrived at 10:45 a.m., Jack admits that he lost his temper.

Particularistic case studies may be instructive but their main purpose is for documentation. The comments that are included in the case study may be used in an instructive manner with the individual who is involved in an attempt to resolve issues or problems. The comments may be used in a memo or letter to the individual that suggests or requires corrective action.

Another type, descriptive case studies, provides thick descriptions of the incident or entity that is being studied. Descriptive studies may be longitudinal or exploratory. No effort is made to develop a theory as the case progresses (Willis, 2007). Descriptive studies include extensive documentation, artifacts, and quotes and illustrate the complexities of a situation such as the fact that not one but many factors contributed to it and show the influence of personalities on the issue. Descriptive case studies may include original documents and artifacts such as interview transcripts, memoranda, email, and newspaper articles. They may also cover many years and describe how a preceding period led to a situation and present diverse viewpoints (Olson in Hoaglin et al., 1982, pp. 138–139).

A descriptive case study may be used to describe an entire institution or the outcomes of one program. A public librarian might use a descriptive study to discuss a summer reading program. This descriptive study might include interviews with parents, children, and librarians. It could include email messages, newspaper articles, photographs, and other artifacts to describe the effectiveness of the summer reading program.

Heuristic case studies are used to solve a research question or a general management problem. Heuristic case studies can be generalized to more than one setting and usually have a heuristic or training quality. Heuristic case studies may be used to resolve library issues involving circulation or reference statistics, budget issues, construction dilemmas, marketing challenges, or to provide training on legal, disability, or multicultural awareness issues.

A case study with heuristic qualities will explain the reasons for a problem, the background of a situation, what happened, and why. If an innovation has been tried, the heuristic study will explain why an innovation worked or failed to work. A heuristic study may discuss and evaluate alternatives (Olson in Hoaglin et al., 1982, pp. 138–139). Heuristic case studies may be based on an issue and are useful for resolving similar issues. They can be used as a form of brainstorming. A library director or department chair may present a brief case study describing a scenario that involves a current library problem or issue and asks all of the participants to write or discuss a solution. An administrator may present a heuristic case study in response to a research question or in trying to understand a problem.

Heuristic case studies typically start with a topical or research question. The topical question is followed by a foreshadowed problem, the foreshadowed problem is thoroughly investigated by researchers, and researchers make logical assertions based on their initial questions. They investigate the issue or problem within a specific environment and supportive documentation.

Heuristic case studies may be useful as teaching tools about legal issues or awareness such as disabilities or multicultural issues. A librarian may present a scenario or case involving a patron with a disability and ask the staff to provide appropriate solutions to the issues that are presented. Copyright issues are sometimes presented as cases in a training session to allow librarians the opportunity to discuss various sections of the copyright laws that are pertinent in libraries and how they should deal with these issues.

A fourth type of case study is collective case study or multiple case study. Other terms commonly applied to this sort of study are multi-case study, multi-site study, cross-case study, and comparative case study. A collective case study involves reviewing a collection of similar cases to determine trends, issues, or problems. Data are collected and synthesized to identify commonalities. Collective case studies are used in performing a program evaluation to provide an accurate picture of the entire organization or program in an effort to compare that program with similar programs at peer or benchmarking institutions. Collective case studies are useful for understanding departmental trends, issues, and problems at similar institutions. For example, a researcher might wish to investigate the effects of serial budget cuts on faculty publications at similar institutions. A collective case study involving ten benchmarking institutions would make a much stronger statement than one case study from one institution. The data from each institution might include lists and types of publications before and after budget cuts, lists of serials and serials databases at each of the institutions, individual interviews, surveys, focus groups and questionnaires for serials librarians, and budget figures. The text will suggest a collective case study approach for the South Central case to discover similar trends, issues, or problems with benchmarking institutions and their information literacy programs.

CASE STUDIES AS HOLISTIC ASSESSMENT

Lincoln and Guba (1985) focus on the case study as a means for reporting observation results. Stake (1978) focused on what is to be accomplished. Whatever the focus, the case study is much more informal and subjective than quantitative designs. Everything that is reported is intended to provide a complex, holistic view of the case. The case study does not just involve observations. The case analysis may include quantitative data, institutional data and records, surveys, interviews, focus groups, and anything that is relevant to the case. A hypothetical program case study that only provides sketchy details will be presented in the next chapter, and we will discuss the mixed methods that will be employed in preparing an actual case and reporting the case analysis. Subsequent chapters will guide you through the process of using these techniques in your own research.

SUMMARY

Case studies may be defined as the process of conducting an investigation as an empirical study (Yin, 2009), a bounded system (Stake, 1995), or the end product (Merriam, 1998). Case studies are particularistic, descriptive, and heuristic, or collective. Researchers have many purposes for using the case study method. They should consider the primary goals or objectives of the research project to determine if the case study method is an appropriate fit for a particular evaluation. The case study method, like any research method, has advantages and disadvantages. The astute researcher will weigh the benefits and problems of the case method and describe the inherent flaws and possible methods for compensating for these flaws in the research process. It is important to understand your case in terms of your disciplinary framework and university setting to provide a sufficient bounding for the case.

APPLICATION QUESTIONS AND EXERCISES

1. Keeping in mind the three purposes of case study research, describe an instance when it might be appropriate to use this method at your library.
2. What are some other uses for case studies other than the ones that Russ-Eft and Preskill identified?
3. Select a topic for case study research.
4. Describe the particular advantages and disadvantages in using the case study method for your research project.

REFERENCES

American Evaluation Association. *Guiding Principles for Evaluators.* Fairhaven, MA: American Evaluation Association, 2004. http://www.eval.org/Publications/GuidingPrinciples .asp.

Charles, C., & Mertler, C. *Introduction to Educational Research.* Boston: Allyn & Bacon, 2004.

Creswell, J. *Qualitative Inquiry and Research Design: Choosing Among Five Traditions.* Thousand Oaks, CA: Sage, 1998.

Creswell, J. *Qualitative Inquiry and Research Design: Choosing Among Five Traditions,* 2nd ed. Thousand Oaks, CA: Sage, 2007.

Cronbach, L., et al. *Toward Reform of Program Evaluation.* San Francisco: Jossey-Bass, 1980.

Denzin, N. *Interpretive Biography.* Qualitative Research Methods 17. Thousand Oaks, CA: Sage, 1989.

Dudden, R. *Using Benchmarking, Needs Assessment, Quality Improvement, Outcome Measurement, and Library Standards.* Medical Library Association Guides. New York: Neal-Schuman, 2007.

Hoaglin, D. C., et al. *Data for Decisions.* Cambridge, MA: Abt Books, 1982.

Lincoln, Y., & Guba, E. *Naturalistic Inquiry.* Thousand Oaks, CA: Sage, 1985.

Marshall, C., & Rossman, G. *Designing Qualitative Research,* 2nd ed. Thousand Oaks, CA: Sage, 1995.

Merriam, S. *Qualitative Research and Case Study Applications in Education*. San Francisco: Jossey-Bass, 1998.

Patton, M. *Qualitative Research and Evaluation Methods*. Thousand Oaks, CA: Sage, 2002.

Powell, R., & Connaway, L. *Basic Research Methods for Librarians*, 4th ed. Library and Information Science Text Series. Westport, CT: Libraries Unlimited, 2004.

Russ-Eft, D., & Preskill, H. *Evaluation in Organizations*. Cambridge, MA: Perseus, 2001.

Sanders, J. Case Study Methodology: A Critique. In W. W. Welsh (ed.), *Case Study Methodology in Educational Evaluation*. Proceedings of the 1981 Minnesota Evaluation Conference. Minneapolis: Minnesota Research and Evaluation Center, 1981.

Stake, R. Case Study Methodology: An Epistemological Advocacy. In W. W. Welsh (ed.), *Case Study Methodology in Educational Evaluation*. Proceedings of the 1981 Minnesota Evaluation Conference. Minneapolis: Minnesota Research and Evaluation Center, 1981.

Stake, R. *The Case Study Method in Social Inquiry*. Thousand Oaks, CA: Sage, 1978.

Stake, R. *The Art of Case Study Research*. Thousand Oaks, CA: Sage, 1995.

Willis, J. *Foundations of Qualitative Research: Interpretive and Critical Approaches*. Thousand Oaks, CA: Sage, 1966.

Wolcott, H. Posturing in Qualitative Inquiry. In M. D. LeCompte, W. L. Millroy, and J. Preissle (eds.), *The Handbook of Qualitative Research in Education*. Orlando, FL: Academic Press, 1992.

Yin, R. The Case Study as a Serious Research Strategy, *Knowledge*, 3 (1981): 97–114.

Yin, R. K. *Case Study Research: Design and Methods*, 4th ed. Thousand Oaks, CA: Sage, 2009.

2

Introduction of the Case Study Method for Program Evaluation

This book focuses on the case study as part of the program evaluation process. While individual case studies are useful for instructional purposes, the greater need in most library settings is for narrative accounts to document outcomes in support of a program, and we will be using a multi-methods approach. A sample case study describing the information literacy curriculum evaluation at South Central University will be used throughout the book to demonstrate this method.

This is not an actual institution or an actual case study. It was chosen to demonstrate a multiple-methods approach, which will provide the most thorough level of data analysis. The case is recorded in first-person form, which is most typical in many case studies; however, it is not always necessary to use first-person language.

This case study is referred to throughout the text to illustrate guidelines, application strategies, and design techniques. Other vignettes are woven into the chapter narratives, but this case study will be one of the primary resources used to apply the case study approach.

This case study is missing several critical pieces as you will discover in exploring each chapter of the text. You will be taking on the job as the program evaluator and it is anticipated that you will be able to point out the deficiencies and to provide the stakeholders with a better focus and a thicker, more thorough description.

While no one approach is necessarily the best, this case study involves inviting someone outside the library to assist with the collection of data and the writing of the report in an orderly manner. An outside consultant usually guarantees objectivity, helps gain a deeper perspective, and ensures inter-rater reliability. In other situations, it is appropriate for an insider to conduct a study. This approach also suggests assembling a group of professionals to accomplish the appropriate tasks. No one approach is necessarily the best. The important thing is to reach consensus on your campus about what approach would be best in your particular setting.

This study is written as a first-person account and the author is selected to conduct the case study analysis because of national recognition in the area of information literacy, familiarity with similar programs, and a strong background in assessment, strengths that a consultant for a study of this nature should possess.

The case study narrative that follows will be in a different font to set this dialogue apart from the remainder of the text. The steps that the researcher takes in this narrative are not necessarily correct or comprehensive. You will work with different sections of this narrative to improve and enhance them as you read each chapter.

The South Central University Information Literacy Curriculum

I had met Jason Norman at the Association of College and Research Librarians (ACRL) conference last spring. Jason was a reference librarian at South Central University. He had attended a panel discussion that I participated in about integrating information literacy skills into the college curriculum. Jason came up to talk to me after the session. He was proud of the information literacy program that he and his colleagues had developed at South Central. Jason's enthusiasm was infectious as he talked about the amazing results that he had seen in the brief pilot period that the course had been offered.

Jason paused at one point and said, "As I mentioned, there is a problem. This is a four-year pilot and some of the faculty members are highly opposed to adding another three-credit-hour course to the curriculum. That is why I wanted to talk to you. I don't know much about assessment and the provost has said that she needs to see something more than a survey. Is there any way that you would be willing to come and help us? We just need to know how to pull the data together and how to convince the faculty that this program is worthwhile. We would like for someone to come from outside just to go over the data that we have collected and to help to make things more convincing."

I suggested that Jason have his library director contact me. Dr. Jane Walters, the library director at South Central, called me the following week. She had already spoken with the provost at South Central about the evaluation. Dr. Porter, the provost, had indicated that she would approve a visit from an outside evaluator. Dr. Walters was contacting me to request that I send a proposal.

Dr. Walters was going to send me a copy of the information literacy curriculum and a brief overview of the program. She seemed vague about details. She simply told me to look over the curriculum and to describe how I would go about evaluating it in my proposal. I took her fuzzy approach to mean that she expected me to indicate my strategy or approach for conducting the evaluation. It was also possible that she was not all that familiar with program evaluation and just wanted me to be a legitimizing voice for her program.

I submitted the proposal addressing the topics that Dr. Walters had mentioned in her conversation with me. Dr. Walters called me a few weeks later and informed me that my proposal had been accepted and she set up a date for me to visit South Central.

When I arrived on campus, the provost, Dr. Anne Porter, invited me to her office and began to chat briefly about the information literacy curriculum. She made it clear that she wanted an objective evaluation of this new information literacy curriculum. "I know you may have visited other universities with better programs. We are proud of the program that we have here but there is always room for improvement. In addition to suggesting improvements, I have to tell you that this program has been highly controversial on our campus. While we have had some perceived gains in academic achievement as a result of this program, this is a required three-credit-hour course. Many faculty members question the logic of adding another three-credit-hour course to the core curriculum when our number of core requirements is already higher than any other state university."

Dr. Porter then produced an agenda for meetings with individuals over the next few days. I would spend the next two days interviewing the library director and the reference librarians who were involved in teaching the information literacy course. On Thursday I would meet with faculty members who had collaborated with the librarians in developing the information literacy course. On Thursday afternoon and Friday I would meet with individual students who had completed the information literacy course. On the following Monday, I would attend a faculty meeting in which the librarians were going to make a presentation based on an assessment that they had completed at the end of the course. A question-and-answer session at the end of this meeting would help the librarians address lingering concerns about the program. I would then wrap up meetings with the library staff and with the provost. I was to return a month later to make a presentation from my data to the Academic Affairs Committee. There would be a brief discussion about the program and then a vote would be taken to determine the fate of the information literacy program at South Central University.

CODES

I will need to establish a list of codes for my field notes. I think that I will wait until I meet with some of the stakeholders before I develop my list.

DOCUMENTS

I contacted Jason Norman and requested access to the information literacy course website so that I could review student papers and projects, and I would need to have the following documents prior to my arrival.

- The survey that Jason had mentioned when I saw him at ACRL
- The pre- and posttest scores from the information literacy course
- LibQUAL results for South Central and their benchmark group
- Copies of the information literacy course evaluations
- A copy of the original course proposal
- A list of all of the faculty, administrators, and support staff who had been involved with developing and teaching the information literacy course with comments about the particular sections of the course that they developed or taught

I contacted Dr. Sanders, the director of institutional research, and requested a copy of a study that he had done with retention data from the cohort that had completed the information literacy course. I contacted Dr. Anderson, the dean of student services, and requested a copy of a study that her department had conducted among students with learning disabilities who had completed the information literacy course. This study involved grade point average data, retention comments, and brief interviews.

TRIANGULATION

I immersed myself in the literature on integrating information literacy into the higher education curriculum. I reviewed the ACRL Information Literacy Standards.

I read Teresa Neely's *Information Literacy Assessment* (Chicago: ALA, 2006). I read Ilene Rockman's *Integrating Information Literacy into the Higher Education Curriculum: Practical Models for Transformation* (San Francisco: Jossey-Bass, 2004) and Dorothy Warner's *A Disciplinary Blueprint for the Assessment of Information Literacy* (Westport, CT: LU, 2008). I read numerous professional journal articles and books on this topic. I developed a list of terms and a corresponding matrix of terms. I asked several librarian colleagues who had recently published in this area if they would be willing to share their curricula, assessment tools, and information literacy website URLs with me. I reviewed library information literacy websites for colleges in Jason's state. I checked with the director of institutional research at South Central and asked for a list of benchmark institutions. I compared information literacy programs for these institutions and requested assessments.

I requested interviews with all of the librarians and faculty who had been involved with developing and teaching the information literacy course. I wanted to get a sense from them of the environment, student achievement, and their individual notion about the utility of the course.

After reviewing the pre- and posttest scores, student papers and projects, I selected twenty students to conduct individual interviews with based on their exemplary work and test score gains. I developed a brief list of interview questions and sent these to Jason for review.

I enlisted the help of the director of institutional research in planning a focus group session that I would conduct while I was on campus. I contacted the dean of student support services concerning the data that she had collected and we decided to collaborate on a follow-up questionnaire. I sent her a pilot copy that she distributed to twelve students who had participated in her study. She administered the pilot version and returned it to me to clarify a couple of items. We would have pizza and invite all of the students to complete the questionnaire while I was on campus.

I would use all of these data to provide the faculty at South Central University with an accurate analysis of the information literacy program. This was going to be an intense week. My goal was to go into the project as an informed professional and to properly inform other professionals about the outcomes of the information literacy course.

3

Evaluating the Proposal

FOCUS QUESTIONS

Who are the potential stakeholders or audience for your evaluation?
How should the potential stakeholders or audience for your evaluation be involved?
Why is it important to describe the goals and objectives of the evaluation?
What tools will you use to describe your case?
Should you consider the political frame or context when conducting your research?

USING AN INTERNAL OR EXTERNAL EVALUATOR

The South Central case study involves an external evaluator who is selected to review a new curriculum. This external evaluator was chosen because of familiarity with similar programs, a national reputation in the area of information literacy in higher education, and a background in assessment.

Whether an assessment occurs internally or externally, there will be certain issues that should be resolved before contacting an outside person or appointing a committee to review the program internally. Ideally, assessment will be considered in the beginning stages of the program. When assessment issues are considered at the beginning of the planning cycle, assessment pieces may be designed as the program develops and the program is complete, which will yield a more consistent and thorough picture than a quick add-on assessment that is designed after the program has been in existence for several years.

The evaluator should determine who is requesting the evaluation, the purpose of the evaluation, the previous planning activities, if a needs assessment has been conducted, the monitoring or assessment instruments that have been developed, and the boundaries or parameters of the program. Find out if any previous evaluation has been done and, if so, when and by whom. The evaluator must know the budget and time constraints involved, the context for the evaluation including the political framework, and if the program is in the preplanning or post-evaluation stage.

DECISION MAKERS

The decision makers will help to determine the parameters, budget, time constraints, and political climate in which the program evaluation will occur. A number of people will be involved in the evaluation process. Typically, there are four groups that you will communicate with and report to as an evaluator: audience, stakeholders, clients, and sponsor. The **audience** includes any of the individuals or groups who will participate in the evaluation as well as anyone who will be reading the final report. The **stakeholders** (anyone who has a vested interest in the evaluation) will include participants as well as administrators, faculty, and library staff. The **client** is the individual or group requesting the evaluation. The **sponsor** is the organization that authorizes the evaluation and provides the budget to support the evaluation plan.

In the South Central case, the **audience** will include students, faculty, librarians, administrators, and anyone else who would need to read or approve the study. The **stakeholders** are anyone who will participate in the study in any way as well as anyone who will approve the study, and the library is the **client**. South Central University would be the **sponsor** for the South Central case study.

PURPOSES OF ASSESSMENT

The general purposes of any assessment activity are to determine if the initial goals and objectives of the program or activity are being met and to determine areas where improvement is necessary. Other general purposes for conducting an evaluation might include stimulating dialog, information gathering for statistical purposes, public relations, or raising awareness of an important issue. Beyond these general purposes, administrators or others in an institution may have specific reasons for conducting an assessment. Some of these reasons might include satisfying requirements for an accreditation visit, addressing recommendations from a previous accreditation team, requesting grant funding, evaluating a program that was funded by a grant, developing a new curriculum or program, addressing a complaint about an existing program, or promoting a highly successful program for political reasons.

It is important for potential outside evaluators to ask questions to determine the exact reasons that they are being asked to conduct an evaluation. Having a clear picture of the purpose of the assessment will enable the consultant to properly tailor any instruments and the final report to address the intended needs.

It is equally important for an internal group to carefully outline its purposes for conducting an evaluation so that it can effectively relate this information to its stakeholders. There should not be ambiguity in the intended purposes for which the assessment will be used. Stufflebeam and Shinkfield (2008) list some typical questions that the audience, stakeholders, clients, and sponsor will wish to answer. Their questions include details about the concept and practice of the program, the program's evolution, program outcomes, disadvantages of the program, values that stakeholders place on the program, reasons for the program's successes or failures, beneficiary's comments about the cost-benefits analysis of the program, program comparisons to similar programs at benchmarking institutions, and universality of the program.

EVALUATION PROCESSES

The initial stages of the program should include the following tools that will be useful throughout the evaluation: conducting a needs assessment, developing goals and objectives appropriate for this activity within this institution, developing the monitoring or assessment instruments, specific boundaries or parameters, comparing the program or benchmarking to similar activities or programs, and planning a budget and time constraints.

Program evaluation that is based on program theory should begin with a well-developed and validated theory based on the literature of programs within similar settings (Stufflebeam & Shinkfield, 2008). For example, with the South Central case, an evaluation should begin with a review of the literature about similar information literacy programs. If no similar program exists, the evaluator must develop a program theory to guide the evaluation.

The process of theory development helps to create an advanced organizer to guide the evaluation. The research questions are then derived from the guiding theory. The theoretical or conceptual framework will help to ground, articulate, and validate the theory. The researcher will ask questions about the program inputs and operations and if they are producing outcomes in the ways the theory predicts. The researcher will want to know what changes in the program's design or implementation might produce better outcomes, if the program is theoretically sound overall, if it operates in accordance with an appropriate theory, and if it can produce the expected outcomes. The researcher will want to know information about the hypothesized causal linkages and whether they have or can be confirmed, what program modifications are needed, if the program is worthy of continuation or dissemination, and what program features are essential for successful replication. (Stufflebeam & Shinkfield, 2008).

According to Stake and others (1994) the major conceptual responsibilities of the case study researcher should be to bound the case as a conceptualized object of study, select phenomena, themes, or issues (the research questions). This person will seek patterns of data to develop the issues, triangulate key observations and bases for interpretation, select alternative interpretations to pursue, and develop assertions or generalizations about the case. These steps help the researcher to refine theory and to interpret results objectively.

Like many program evaluators, Provus (1973) viewed evaluation as a process that should begin in the early stages of program development. He noted five stages of program development beginning with the *definition* or program design stage in his Discrepancy Evaluation Model. During the design stage, goals, processes, activities, and resources are determined or at least considered.

Installation is the next stage in the Provus model. The design is implemented during this stage at least in a pilot form. The stakeholders determine what modifications or revisions need to be made to the program to make it more effective or efficient.

The next two stages are *process* and *product*. The *process* stage occurs when the stakeholders determine whether short-term objectives are being met. During the *product* stage decisions are made to see if the long-term objectives or outcomes are being met by the program.

A final stage of the Provus model is the *analysis*. In this stage, the evaluator performs a cost-benefit analysis and compares the results with similar programs of benchmarking institutions.

Theory-based program evaluation is a process that is outlined by program experts with knowledge about how a program is expected to operate and produce results. Flow-charts and other graphics may be used to determine inputs and outcomes. Interviews, observations, and university documents are collected in support of the program. Grounded theory is often used in theory-based program evaluation to observe events and analyze materials (Stufflebeam & Shinkfield, 2008).

Robert Stake (1995) provides a useful list of criteria for rating a case study proposal. Stake's checklist evaluates areas of communication, content, method, and practicality.

SELECTING AN EVALUATOR

Once the purposes of the assessment have been determined, the next task is to select appropriate evaluators for the program. As suggested earlier, Fitzpatrick, Sanders, and Worthen (2004) agree that selecting an outside evaluator to conduct the summative evaluation has advantages in that he or she is more likely to be impartial, perhaps more credible, may have a higher degree of evaluation expertise, and is not involved with campus politics. Some of the advantages of internal evaluations would be a greater knowledge and familiarity with the program model and its history, greater familiarity with various stakeholders, and the dynamics of organizational decision making. Internal evaluators will continue to serve as advocates for the findings of the study after it is completed and the stakeholders are aware of an internal evaluator's strengths and weaknesses.

Combining the use of internal experts and external consultants is another approach that is often used, especially with formal program evaluations. This approach generally involves an institutional or departmental self-study in which the on-campus experts review the activity or program and address its strengths and weaknesses before calling an outside consultant or team of experts. Each method has disadvantages and when the two are combined effectively, an institution can save resources and appease stakeholders. The consistency and stability provided by this approach will ensure that needed modifications are accomplished in a timely manner after the assessment is complete.

After the institution's representatives have decided whether they will use an internal or external evaluator or a combination of the two, they must then decide the qualifications or specific areas of expertise that this individual(s) must have. If an external evaluator is to be invited to participate in the analysis, someone within the institution will contact a specific individual or will issue a request for proposals (RFP) for the project.

The group should ask some of the following questions in the process of selecting an appropriate evaluator:

- Is a potential evaluator considered an expert in the area of the activity that is being evaluated?
- Has this person published, presented at professional conferences, or had experience in this area?
- Is the potential evaluator trained in using the methodologies and technologies that may be used in this evaluation?
- Is the potential evaluator a good communicator?
- Does this person have the verbal and written communication skills necessary to articulate the focus and results of the evaluation?
- Is it likely this person would be a good trainer?

- Is the potential evaluator a good manager, can meet deadlines, and will work to coordinate all facets of the evaluation?
- Is the potential evaluator an ethical person?

Obviously an affirmative response is needed to all of the above questions.

CASE APPLICATION

I had more questions than answers after my meeting with Dr. Porter. I wondered why they had not considered an evaluation of the program in the beginning planning stages. I wondered why Dr. Porter was not more specific about the data that were available. Was she not aware of any internal data? Had there not been any surveys, interviews, pretests, or posttests? I thought that Jason had mentioned a retention study that the Dean of Students had conducted with learning disabilities students. The LibQUAL survey results were not available when I requested them from Dr. Walters. Dr. Sanders seemed to be evasive about the retention data from benchmarking institutions. I was excited about this evaluation when I came on campus but now I am beginning to believe that I was brought in to do a quick report of the information literacy program that will be filed away and never used. One of the librarians made a comment in the break room this morning that I tried to ignore. He said, "They're always bringing these consultants in to do evaluations and then they never do anything with their reports. They do not want this three-hour information literacy course for sure and they are just trying to use you to prove their point. Besides Dr. Walters always gives in to Dr. Porter anyway. She's not going to bite the hand that feeds her."

I am beginning to wonder if I will be able to navigate the political waters on the South Central campus to get the data that I need to develop a fair and ethical report. I know from previous experience that sometimes breaking the ice can be a challenge. Should I continue with the evaluation? They have not given me a contract yet. I desperately need to see the terms of the contract and to seek more clarification about the cooperation that I will have from the stakeholders.

I have noticed that both Drs. Walters and Porter do not like me mentioning other information literacy studies or experts in the field. I am also suspicious about my carefully outlined schedule. I wonder what stakeholders participated in developing the schedule. I wonder why I am meeting with some of the individuals on my list and why I am not scheduled to meet with other individuals that I would consider to be key players in the process. Do you have some suggestions about how I might answer some of these questions and deal with the political dilemmas that I am sure to face?

APPLICATION QUESTIONS AND EXERCISES

1. An acquisitions librarian has just sent you an email requesting that you do a productivity evaluation for her department. What questions would you ask?
2. Should you decline some requests even if you are an expert in the area that you are being asked to evaluate? Why?

3. Consider a library program or department with which you are familiar. Would an internal or external person be best suited to conduct this study?
4. What are some advantages and disadvantages of having an evaluation conducted by an external person? By an internal person?
5. What criteria would you use to select an external evaluator?
6. What questions should you ask before agreeing to perform an evaluation?
7. What knowledge and skills would be necessary to evaluate the information literacy program at South Central University?
8. What criteria would you consider in hiring an evaluator for this program?

MAJOR CHAPTER THEMES

As an evaluator you will be expected to communicate with a general audience, individual stakeholders, the client, and the evaluation sponsor. Involve each of these groups or individuals at each stage of the evaluation process.

A thorough understanding of the purpose of the proposed evaluation will help you to function effectively as an evaluator at each stage of the evaluation process.

Determining the value of conducting an assessment is useful both for the organization and for the potential evaluator at the outset.

Either an internal or external evaluator may conduct an evaluation. It is sometimes productive to use both. Internal evaluators bring more internal knowledge and background to the evaluation. External evaluators tend to be perceived as being neutral and objective.

Selecting an appropriate evaluator involves considering candidates' credentials. They must be an expert in the field, a good manager, and an experienced communicator.

CHAPTER EVALUATION STANDARDS

Review the Joint Committee on Standards for Educational Evaluation (1994) in Appendix A. Describe the standards that are relevant to this chapter.

REFERENCES

Fitzpatrick, J., Sanders, J., & Worthen, B. *Program Evaluation: Alternative Approaches and Practical Guidelines*, 3rd ed. Boston: Allyn & Bacon, 2004.

Joint Committee on Standards for Educational Evaluation. *The Program Evaluation Standards*, 2nd ed. Thousand Oaks: Sage, 1994.

Provus, M. *Discrepancy Evaluation*. Berkeley, CA: McCutchan, 1973.

Stake, R. *The Art of Case Study Research*. Thousand Oaks, CA: Sage, 1995.

Stake, R. Case studies. In N. K. Denzin & Y. S. Lincoln (Eds.), *Handbook of Qualitative Research* (pp. 236–247). Thousand Oaks: Sage, 1994.

Stake, R. Responsive evaluation. Unpublished manuscript, 1972.

Stufflebeam, D., & Shinkfield, A. *Evaluation Theory, Models, and Applications*. San Francisco, CA: Jossey-Bass, 2008.

4

Evaluation Designs

FOCUS QUESTIONS

Why is it important to be aware of different evaluation designs?
What are the advantages and disadvantages of the different evaluation designs?
Would it be appropriate to combine any of these designs?

CLASSIFICATION SCHEMA DESIGN

Fitzpatrick, Sanders, and Worthen (2004) developed a **classification schema design** for evaluation approaches that is helpful in determining the approach that you will take in your particular situation. Their schema includes the following:

1. *Objectives-oriented design:* This approach focuses on defining goals and objectives and measuring progress toward achieving the predetermined goals and objectives.
2. *Management-oriented design:* The main concern is to provide information for managers.
3. *Consumer-oriented design:* The focus is on developing products and services that measure accountability.
4. *Expertise-oriented design:* This approach depends on professionals to assess the quality of a product or service.
5. *Participant-oriented design:* This approach involves participants in the evaluation process. The participants develop the design for the evaluation and are responsible for collecting and interpreting the results.

OBJECTIVES-ORIENTED DESIGN

Determining Objectives in the Values, Criteria-Oriented Approach is an **objectives-oriented design** and was first championed by Tyler (1950) in the 1930s. This "Management by Objectives" approach has been used in business as well as education. Various logic models have been applied using a similar approach in science and engineering fields. An objectives-oriented evaluation focuses on a set of objectives and the extent to which these objectives are met. The information gained from an objectives-oriented evaluation can be used to refine an activity as well as to evaluate actual outcomes. Tyler (1950) advocated for seven steps in an objectives-oriented evaluation.

1. Establish broad goals or objectives.
2. Classify the goals or objectives.
3. Define objectives in behavioral terms.
4. Find a situation in which achievement of objectives can be shown.
5. Develop or select measurement techniques.
6. Collect performance data.
7. Compare performance data with behaviorally stated objectives.

Discrepancies in the cycle would be noted and deficiencies would be corrected. Tyler encouraged the use of broad goals instead of behavioral objectives initially because he thought that objectives would be restrictive in the initial stages of program development. Tyler thought that the broader goals could be screened during the pilot phases of program development and then refined before they were developed into behavioral objectives and accepted as part of the evaluation strategy.

Metfessel and Michael (1967) enlarged the application of Tyler's model to include alternative instruments such as documents, artifacts, and case study applications with an objectives-based approach. Their evaluation model suggested involving stakeholders to facilitate program evaluation, formulating goals and objectives, selecting instruments to measure program effectiveness, observations using content-valid tests, scales, and other behavioral measures, analyzing data, interpreting data using standards of performance, and developing recommendations for further implementation, modification, and revision of broad goals and objectives.

Advantages of the Objectives-Oriented Evaluation Design

The main advantage of the objectives-oriented evaluation design is the simplicity of developing measurable behavior objectives, developing content to teach the objectives, teaching the outlined content, and testing based on the objectives. This method can clearly be understood and interpreted by all of the stakeholders.

Disadvantages of the Objectives-Oriented Evaluation Design

"Teaching for the test" has been a major criticism of the standardized test movement in the public schools and in education in general in recent years. Fitzpatrick, Sanders, and Worthen (2004) assert that the objectives-oriented evaluation design does not have sufficiently comprehensive evaluative measures. This method needs criteria for measuring the importance of discrepancies between objectives and performance levels, does not assign specific values to objectives, may not consider alternatives in the planning process, does not consider the context for the evaluation, and may not provide for unintended outcomes. Program data may be deleted if not perceived as directly relevant to the program objectives and this design tends to promote a linear evaluation approach. The objectives-oriented evaluation design can result in tunnel vision, limiting the effectiveness and potential of the program and of the evaluation.

MANAGEMENT-ORIENTED EVALUATION DESIGN

The **management-oriented evaluation** design is best suited for decision makers. The management-oriented approach is a systems or logic approach and depends heavily on inputs, processes, and outputs. The management-oriented approach delineates who will be using the evaluation results and how they will be used. The decision maker's criteria and concerns are woven into the evaluation.

Stufflebeam (1968) developed the context, input, process, and product (CIPP) model. He made the concerns of the decision makers the main organizer for the program evaluation rather than a set of behavioral objectives. The CIPP model is intended to help administrators and decision makers in making four types of decisions: context evaluation or planning decisions, input evaluation or structuring decisions, process evaluation or implementation decisions, and product evaluation or closing the loop assessments. Stufflebeam (1973) suggests a protocol for program evaluators that includes specific steps for focusing the evaluation, collecting, organizing, analyzing, and reporting information, and administering the evaluation.

Yin (2009) insists that having a case study, protocol especially with a multiple-case study, is essential for helping the researcher to carry out the data collection from a single case to multiple cases with reliable results. Alkin (1969) developed a similar system evaluation model. These models are more linear in scope. However, Stufflebeam's focus on the context grounds his model in a more holistic framework. The CIPP model has been used for program improvement and accountability.

Advantages of the Management-Oriented Evaluation Design

Most administrators and decision makers like the straightforward aspect of the management-oriented evaluation design. The questions, issues, and problems are determined by the decision makers, and this approach has a clear focus or purpose. The management-oriented evaluation design supports the evaluation needs of the program from initial baseline data and can begin in the earliest stages of the program process and continue through final assessments. The evaluator can identify a set of questions for each of the four stages of the CIPP model. The CIPP model stresses timely feedback to decision makers.

Disadvantages of the Management-Oriented Evaluation Design

The management-oriented evaluation design depends on close teamwork with administrators, decision makers, and the evaluator. The administrators or decision makers are responsible for giving the evaluator a clear focus. The evaluator is given the task of providing a clear plan based on the questions and issues provided by the decision makers. Feedback from both parties is essential at every stage. If decision makers do not provide a clear focus, the evaluator will not be able to conduct an effective and relevant management-oriented evaluation. Another disadvantage is that the management-oriented evaluation approach leaves no place for anyone other than administrators or decision makers within the organization to participate in the evaluation process. This is a top-down management approach. Only managers and decision makers participate.

CONSUMER-ORIENTED EVALUATION DESIGN

The **consumer-oriented evaluation** design is one with which most of us are familiar. Every product or service has a consumer evaluation component these days. Some of the items that we evaluate in libraries might include new technology, software, equipment, inservice training programs, media, supplies, and other services and materials. Additionally, we evaluate staff performance individually and as part of various program evaluations. Many checklists are available from library resources, education, and other consumer-based evaluation sources for evaluating any type of service, product, or program.

The Curriculum Materials Analysis System (CMAS) checklist developed by Morrisett and Stevens (1967) provides useful guidelines for product analysis. Their list includes specific details on describing product characteristics, analyzing the rationale and objectives, considering the conditions in using this product, considering product content and instructional theory, and forming overall judgments.

Advantages of the Consumer-Oriented Evaluation Design

The consumer-oriented evaluation design is generally simple to administer in the form of a checklist, Likert scale, or short survey or evaluation form. Familiarity with consumer-based evaluations helps stakeholders to readily accept evaluations of this type. They provide an important accountability check and assure the consumer or patron that the library is interested in participant opinions. Checklists for expensive technology, software, and other materials help the librarian to make responsible purchases and to avoid wasting scarce funds. The consumer-oriented evaluation design asks questions about process information, content information, transportability, and effectiveness information. Specific questions in each of these areas help the evaluator to make accurate, informed, and responsible decisions.

Disadvantages of the Consumer-Oriented Evaluation Design

The consumer-oriented evaluation approach has few disadvantages. One possible disadvantage is that it might be overused. Patrons and library staff may tend not to take checklists and evaluation forms seriously if they are administered too frequently.

EXPERTISE-ORIENTED EVALUATION DESIGNS

Expertise-oriented evaluation designs involve inviting an expert in a particular field or subject area to come to your library or gather information to assess a program or activity. In some cases, a team of experts may be involved with the assessment. Some examples of expertise-oriented evaluation approaches would include professional reviews conducted by professional accreditation teams, national licensing review boards, staff performance reviews, promotion and tenure review committees, peer reviews of potential professional journal articles, and site visits to evaluate grant-sponsored programs. These visits may include a formal professional protocol or review or they may be more informal or even ad hoc.

An accreditation visit would be an example of a formal review. You will have documents prepared for the visiting team in anticipation that they will request artifacts to substantiate facts and figures that are presented in your report. Promotion and tenure reviews, similarly, would be formal expert reviews for which you would have prior knowledge of the documentation and artifacts that you should deliver and you would prepare those documents for the committee. Sometimes the library may be included in an ad hoc fashion in a site visit for a grant-sponsored activity or program.

In most cases, there are no standards or objectives to prepare your library for an assessment. Most assessments are subjective. The best practice in most areas is to compare your data with benchmarking institutions. Documentation of continuous improvement and closing the loop are always compelling evidence.

Advantages of the Expertise-Oriented Evaluation Design

Kirkwood (1982) discusses the benefits of the expertise-oriented evaluation approach. These benefits include fostering excellence by developing guidelines to assess institutional effectiveness, continuous improvement, and protecting institutional rights and freedoms.

Disadvantages of the Expertise-Oriented Evaluation Design

Some institutions do not make a consistent effort to provide continuous improvement and attempt to create an appearance of competency before an expert team is scheduled to visit. Preparing for an expert or a team visit is costly in terms of staff time and financial resources. It is difficult for any one person or team to adequately assess a large program or complex activity in a brief visit.

PARTICIPANT-ORIENTED EVALUATION DESIGNS

Participant-oriented evaluation designs focus on serving the program participants as opposed to the administrators or stakeholders. Stake (1967) was one of the earliest proponents of participant-oriented evaluation.

Stake (1972) discusses two different types of case study evaluation: **responsive evaluation** and **preordinate evaluation**. **Responsive evaluation** is what we do naturally— observe and react. **Responsive evaluation** focuses on training the researcher to observe and to be responsive to the reactions, concerns, and issues of the program and of the stakeholders.

Preordinate evaluation focuses on a prescribed evaluation plan and does not go beyond the predetermined issues and predefined problems. Fitzpatrick, Sanders, and Worthen (2004) list commonalities or characteristics that are a part of the participant-oriented evaluation design. The participant-oriented approach depends on inductive reasoning, uses a multiplicity of data, does not follow a standard plan, and records multiple rather than single realities.

Stake (1967) spoke of two basic acts of evaluation: *description* and *judgment*. He referred to these acts or phases as the "two countenances" of evaluation. This framework provides a "thick" description (meaning giving the whole story) of the program activities and outcomes. A thick description might include interviews, focus group data, survey results, internal documents, benchmarking data, photographs, and any other documents that help the reader to understand the case as a whole. In contrast, quantitative data simply provide a set of numbers. Just a survey, for example, will leave the reader with more questions than answers.

The countenance provides a theoretical framework for considering data in a holistic fashion. Improved communication with stakeholders as well as participants is the main goal of the participant-oriented evaluation design.

Guba and Lincoln (1981) discuss the triangulation of naturalistic inquiry with other data sources to cross-check the findings for internal validity in a holistic inquiry for participant-oriented evaluations. The data collection task is defined through interviews, observations, nonverbal cues, documents, records, and unobtrusive measures.

Advantages of the Participant-Oriented Evaluation Design

The participant-oriented evaluation design clearly emphasizes the human element in evaluation. It is a holistic approach and includes the strengths or advantages of all of the methods that we have discussed.

Disadvantages of the Participant-Oriented Evaluation Design

Some evaluators argue that the participant-oriented evaluation design is too subjective to be considered valid. It is more labor intensive and costly than some other methods.

APPLICATION QUESTIONS AND EXERCISES

1. Consider an evaluation that you have been a part of in the past. This may have been a performance evaluation or something more formal when you were involved in evaluating an activity or program.
   a. What was the purpose of this evaluation?
   b. What methods were used?
   c. Who was involved with the evaluation?
   d. What data were collected?
   e. How were these data used?
   f. What approach was used in this evaluation?
2. Consider a program or activity with which you are familiar.
   a. What evaluation design would you use to evaluate that program or activity? Why?
   b. What are the major strengths of the design that you have selected?
   c. What are the major weaknesses of the design that you have selected?
   d. What types of data will you collect for your evaluation?
   e. What questions might stakeholders ask for your evaluation?

MAJOR CHAPTER THEMES

Ralph Tyler was the first proponent of the objectives-oriented design to evaluation. Tyler used the objectives as standards to evaluate whether or not a program was successful or deficient in certain areas.

Daniel Stufflebeam developed the context, input, process, and product (CIPP) model for program evaluation upon which the management-oriented evaluation approach is based. This model primarily serves decision makers in forming policy and evaluating administrative processes and provides information on available resources, alternative strategies, and possible plans.

Consumer-oriented evaluations primarily serve the consumer. They point to more effective product development and services.

Expert-oriented evaluations indicate proficiency in a given field or activity. Professional judgment is the main gauge for program effectiveness. Tenure committees, accreditation teams, and journal peer reviewers are examples of expert-oriented evaluations.

Participant-oriented evaluations seek to provide a holistic picture for the audience, stakeholders, client, and sponsor. Participant-oriented evaluations describe the purposes, goals, and objectives of the program and indicate the effectiveness of these standards. This holistic picture helps everyone who will be reviewing the evaluation report to clearly judge the program's effectiveness and utility.

CHAPTER EVALUATION STANDARDS

Review the Joint Committee on Standards for Educational Evaluation (1994) in Appendix A. Describe the standards that are relevant to this chapter.

REFERENCES

Alkin, M. Evaluation Theory Development. *Evaluation Comment, 2* (1969): 2–7.

Fitzpatrick, J., Sanders, J., & Worthen, B. *Program Evaluation: Alternative Approaches and Practical Guidelines*, 3rd ed. Boston: Allyn & Bacon, 2004.

Guba, E., & Lincoln, Y. *Effective Evaluation*. San Francisco: Jossey-Bass, 1981.

Kirkwood, R. Accreditation. In H. E. Mitzel (ed.), *Encyclopedia of Educational Research*, 1, 5th ed. New York: Macmillan, 1982.

Metfessel, N., & Michael, W. A Paradigm Involving Multiple Criterion Measures for the Evaluation of the Effectiveness of School Programs. *Educational and Psychological Measurement, 27* (1967): 931–943.

Morrisett, I., & Stevens, W. *Steps in Curriculum Analysis Outline*. Boulder, CO: Social Science Education Consortium, 1967.

Stake, R. The Countenance of Educational Evaluation. *Teacher's College Record*, 68(1967): 523–540.

Stake, R. Responsive Evaluation. Unpublished manuscript. 1972.

Stufflebeam, D. *Evaluation as Enlightenment for Decision Making*. Columbus: Ohio State University Evaluation Center, 1968.

Stufflebeam, D. Excerpts from "Evaluation as Enlightenment for Decision-Making." In B. Worthen & J. Sanders (Eds.), *Educational Evaluation: Theory and Practice*. Belmont, CA: Wadsworth, 1973.

Tyler, R. *Basic Principles of Curriculum and Instruction*. Chicago: University of Chicago Press, 1950.

Yin, R. *Case Study Research: Design and Methods*, 4th ed. Thousand Oaks, CA: Sage, 2009.

5

Bounding the Case Study and
Analyzing the Context

FOCUS QUESTIONS

What is the context of the program?
Who are the stakeholders for the evaluation?
What is to be evaluated?
What is the conceptual framework of the program?
What methods will you use to describe the program?

An individual or particularistic case study may begin with a description of the person and a general statement concerning the problem behaviors that this person is presenting in his or her environment. Studies involving a program or activity may begin with a general statement about the perceived problem(s) within this program or activity. Instrumental case studies may begin with a general statement of the problem, issue, or training that is under consideration.

The problem definition and the initial descriptors provide background information to answer the *what* and *how* questions connected with the case. This background information gives the reader a sense of the problem and the environment. The problem definition and case description may also establish focal points and boundaries about cases and sub-cases to be studied. The program description includes goals and objectives, critical components and activities, and descriptions of the target audience. The program description may include contextual information about the physical setting, characteristics of program personnel, and program needs.

THE CONCEPTUAL FRAMEWORK

Fitzpatrick, Sanders, and Worthen (2004) suggest developing a list of questions to determine the conceptual framework for the evaluation. This list should include program items such as needs, components, context, stakeholders, history, and resources.

Most experts agree that a program evaluator should communicate to the stakeholders that a program is not ready for a formal evaluation if the program description is not clear. The conceptual framework provides a firm scaffold for the program and little can be determined about the program's effectiveness if this framework has not been firmly established.

PROGRAM THEORY

Program theory is largely derived from current literature on a given topic or program, expert opinion, and benchmarking. These sources provide the evaluator with best practices in the field and standards by which to judge them. Benchmarking helps to provide valid measures for inputs and outputs. The stakeholders may have already developed a program theory based on the literature and may have already prepared some benchmarking data. If not, the program evaluator will want to provide these resources.

PROGRAM DESCRIPTION

The program description should include descriptive documents, interviews, and observations. Descriptive documents might include such items as planning documents, program reports, meeting minutes, publications, email, and letters describing the program. Interviews with stakeholders and participants give the program evaluator a deeper description of the program. Actual observations help the program evaluator to understand any differences between written documents and actual performance or outputs.

SAMPLING

It is sometimes difficult to determine which cases would be most representative of the whole when conducting a program evaluation. The program evaluator wants to select a sufficient sample to increase generalizability to the entire population.

Patton (1990) suggested fifteen strategies for selecting sampling types. The most common sampling involves selecting critical cases, extreme cases, typical cases, and varied cases. The logic and power of probability sampling depends on selecting a random and statistically representative sample that will justify generalizations to a larger population. However, the power and logic of purposeful sampling lies in selecting information-rich cases for in-depth study. For example, if the purpose of the case study is to determine the relevance of a new chemistry database for chemistry students, the researcher will want a purposeful sample that accurately represents this group and may select ten chemistry PhD students for interviews. The following strategies are suggested by Patton (1990) in selecting purposeful samples for information-rich cases. I have added examples of library applications for each strategy.

Extreme or Deviant Case Sampling

These cases are either outstanding failures or successes. Down and Out Library in Poorville, USA, is located in a section of town where gang activity was rampant. Children never came to the library. Karen Jones moved to Poorville and accepted a job as the library director. Karen immediately decided that she was going to change her environment. She went to visit the local probation officer and asked him to set up interviews with some of the gang members in the neighborhood. After completing a series of interviews, Karen completed her case analysis and determined that she would start a literacy program for young teens. She had learned from her data the materials that would be most appropriate for this group, the incentives that would be most appealing to them, and had established a rapport with these individuals.

Intensity Sampling

Intensity sampling is less extreme than deviant sampling. It is often used in heuristic research to describe phenomenon or emotions. For example, a case study researcher might wish to do a study on feelings of isolation and loneliness among mid-level library managers. The researcher would select a group of mid-level library managers and might either interview them individually and/or ask them to complete a survey about isolation and loneliness issues. The researcher might cross-analyze the results and determine the prevalence of feelings of loneliness and isolation among mid-level managers and might perhaps suggest some strategies for overcoming these problems.

Maximum Variation Sampling

Maximum variation sampling is used particularly in impact studies to capture central themes and principal outcomes. Common patterns that emerge using this technique are of particular interest to the researcher. The value is in capturing the core experiences and the shared aspects or impacts of a program. For example, Bob might be evaluating a nationwide library program. Bob decides that he will contact library directors that are members of ACRL and visit twenty of these librarians and interview them about this program. These twenty librarians are all from different states so that Bob will have adequate variation in sampling. Bob will not take these results and generalize the results to a national population but will instead look for information that identifies programmatic variation and significant common patterns within that variation.

Homogeneous Samples

Homogeneous sampling is the opposite of maximum variation sampling. The point of homogeneous sampling is to describe a particular subgroup in detail. Focus groups are typically homogeneous groups that examine issues using open-ended questions in a group interview setting. A case study researcher, Jane, might conduct a focus group with a group of college seniors that have never used the library. Jane would use the data from this group interview to determine underlying causes for library apathy among this group and possible solutions for this problem.

Typical Case Sampling

Typical cases are selected by key informants, program staff, and knowledgeable participants. These individuals can identify what is "typical." Typical cases may also be selected electronically using software to find averages and modal scores from survey data. The purpose of reporting typical cases is to illustrate or define what is typical to someone who may not be familiar with a program. For example, the manufacturer of a new copier designed for large books that automatically turns the pages may be interested in conducting a series of case studies with a group of "typical" libraries across the

United States. They ask Mr. Don Charming to select fifty typical libraries. Mr. Charming reviews usage data from his current customer list and identifies fifty libraries that make an average number of copies per year. He contacts these libraries and sets up his new copiers at these sites. He agrees to allow these libraries to have a thirty-day free trial of the copier in exchange for keeping an observation log in which they record problems and patron comments and participate in an in-depth interview with Mr. Charming himself at the end of the thirty days. Mr. Charming will use these data to identify problems with the copier and customer satisfaction.

Stratified Purposeful Sampling

Stratified purposeful sampling involves selecting layers or strata to examine variations. Stratified purposeful sampling may be considered a thicker, more in-depth version of maximum variation sampling. Instead of having one person from a certain category, you may interview five people from each category. The purpose of this technique is to identify commonalities among groups such as socioeconomic or political groups. These groups are typically too small to generalize the results to a larger population but they do identify common issues that may be useful for further testing.

Critical Case Sampling

Critical cases make a dramatic point. Typically a key informant provides observation data to indicate that if an event occurred in this setting, it could happen anywhere. Diane McWhirley, a library director at Midville College, was astounded to hear that a reference librarian at Midwestern Bible College had recently shot her close friend, Tina Walters, the library director, two other librarians, and several students before shooting himself. She had visited Tina on several occasions at Midwestern and had always remarked about the calm, serene setting. Tina's small staff all seemed like family. Diane could not imagine that such an awful tragedy could have occurred at Midwestern. Diane contacted the vice president for academic affairs at Midwestern and asked if she could interview the librarians at Midwestern Bible College. Diane wants to make sense of this situation because she is convinced that if such a tragedy could have occurred at Midwestern, it could happen anywhere. Diane will look for anything that might explain the bizarre behavior of the individual who committed this act. She will also be concerned with potential solutions that the librarians might have for preventing this sort of tragedy on other campuses.

Critical cases are used to demonstrate potential effectiveness. For example, if a library with extremely limited funds has a highly effective program, a researcher might conclude that any library could deliver similar results based on the cost-per-student ratio.

Snowball or Chain Sampling

This process involves contacting key informants and asking to talk with experts on a given topic. The process starts with a question such as, "Who should I talk to about . . . " or "Who knows a lot about . . . " The snowball gets bigger and bigger as one person mentions an expert and that expert in turn mentions someone else. Tom wants to research the effectiveness of a new assistive technology in libraries.

Tom contacts his friend, Joe Lazzaro, who wrote *Adaptive Technologies for Learning and Work Environments*. Joe agrees to meet with Tom for an interview. Joe talks to Tom about his experiences with this new technology and then suggests that Tom should meet his friend Norm Coombs at Rochester Institute of Technology.

Tom contacts Norm and Norm agrees to meet with Tom for an interview. Norm then suggests that Tom should meet with Jeromy Elkind at Kurzweil. Tom contacts Jeromy and he agrees to meet with him for an interview. Tom continues to meet with another ten people who tell him about their experiences with using this new assistive technology based on their individual areas of expertise. They all identify certain areas of weakness in their expertise but recommend other experts who can fill in these gaps. Tom is able to gain a holistic picture of the effectiveness of this technology by interviewing all of these experts.

Peters and Waterman's (1984) study *In Search of Excellence* began with snowball sampling. *The Change Masters* (Robert Kanter, 1983) is another example of a study that utilized this technique.

Criterion Sampling

Criterion sampling is typically used when a phenomenon cannot be explained for a given case or for one group or program. Janice and Carl have taught an information skills class for the last five years. They have always been proud of their posttest scores because they have been significantly higher than the pretest scores. This semester, Janice and Carl are puzzled by one set of scores. One entire class scored lower on the posttest scores than they had scored on the pretest. They remember that this group was unusually attentive and appeared to be engaged in the learning process. They decide to interview twelve students from this class to get in-depth responses about the problems with these scores.

Theory-Based or Operational Construct Sampling

The researcher samples incidents, time periods, or people based on important theoretical constructs. These constructs or entities are usually legally or financially defined. An operational construct is a real-world example and the study of several examples that fit within this construct would be considered "multiple operationalism."

Catherine decides that she is going to study ADA compliance issues in academic libraries in her state. She reviews Title III of the ADA and develops a compliance matrix. She then develops a questionnaire based on this matrix and posts it on the discussion list for her state library organization. These steps will help Catherine to develop a theoretical construct.

Catherine decides to visit all of the academic libraries whose librarians have responded to the questionnaire to conduct in-depth interviews with the library directors and other librarians who are involved with providing special services. She has made the leap to multiple operationalism. Catherine will use responses from the questionnaire, some research questions that she has developed, and some hunches from her observations to form her interview questions. Catherine collects brochures, URLs, policy statements, product literature, surveys from patrons with special needs, and other documentation to corroborate her field notes.

Catherine established codes for recording her field notes before she began the interviews. She will transfer her coded data from her field notes to the matrices that she developed at the beginning of the process. She will review her completed matrices and all of her data and will make appropriate judgments about ADA compliance issues at academic libraries in her state.

Confirming and Disconfirming Cases

The act of finding and reporting data from confirming as well as disconfirming cases involves extreme rigor on the part of the researcher. Confirming cases fit already established categories or emerging patterns. These cases further confirm findings and add richness and depth. Disconfirming cases are the outliers. Disconfirming cases are the exceptions to the rule. While disconfirming cases may not serve to validate the case, they do serve to confirm the credibility of the researcher and often provide a source for further research and investigation. Steve Milligan has just returned from a conference where he attended a session on disability awareness trainings. He was particularly interested in one training presentation because it involved a library similar in size and scope to his library. The library director cited impact results that indicated that this program had been highly successful at her library. Steve talked with her after the session and she agreed to send him all of her training materials and to come to his library for the training. As Steve talked with her, she proudly told him about students with learning disabilities who had become engaged in library research because the reference librarians now knew how to address their specific disabilities.

She also told stories about students with print disabilities that were using the Kurzweil software and other tools to accomplish their research and who were making significant academic gains. She mentioned that they had moved all of the assistive technology out to the middle of the library so that it would be easily accessible for patrons, and library staff could easily see when someone needed help with the equipment. Then she said, "Perhaps I shouldn't mention this, but we have had one very disappointing dilemma. After we moved all of the assistive technology out in the middle of the library we noticed that one girl who had come to the library regularly to use the Kurzweil quit coming. One of our reference librarians saw her on campus and she said that she felt totally humiliated to sit where everyone could see her reading large print on a screen out in the middle of the library. Another young man with a hearing problem reported that he would no longer use the TTY machine because it was in the middle of the library."

Steve has just been told about two disconfirming cases. He asked the library director if she could give him contact information for these individuals so that he can get some further information from them about how to develop a more inclusive and yet private environment for patrons with disabilities at his library.

Opportunistic Sampling

While case study research should be structured to some extent; it is good to remain open to new opportunities. You will meet individuals in the course of your interview or observation that you had not planned to interview but who may have significant data or experiences to add to the study. You may determine later that it is not appropriate to include these impromptu interviews. It is better to take the risk and decide that you will not need or cannot use the information later than to neglect mining some gem that may shed an important light on the case.

Carol is interviewing technical services librarians regarding a new systems project that they have initiated. The librarians invite her to the library café for coffee and the director of campus systems support joins them. He immediately begins to talk about the new Oracle-based system and some of the challenges that he faces in trying to migrate current data and to interface this system with the current network. Carol had not planned to interview him but she decides that perhaps he might fill in some gaps regarding the technology that the librarians have not answered.

Purposeful Random Sampling

Random sampling may be used in qualitative research as well as quantitative. Impact studies or "war" stories are sometimes the most effective technique for demonstrating effectiveness. However, this technique can be made more credible using randomized sampling.

War stories demonstrate effectiveness after the fact. Purposeful random sampling seeks to select potential participants randomly based on a set of predetermined criteria. Using this technique, the researcher establishes a set list of criteria for participants and has participants complete a questionnaire to determine if they are an appropriate fit for the study. Shamika is trying a new women's studies database in the reference department for thirty days. She talked with the women's studies professor and asked her to bring her class to the library for training the first week that the database was available. Shamika has noticed that this professor has told several of her friends about the database and they have come in to use it. Also, word seems to have circulated among the students about the new database.

Shamika has been asked to do a training session for an English class so that they can use the database for a research paper on women authors. Shamika knows that this database is expensive and that she will need to make a powerful statement to her director to persuade her to provide the funding for this new database.

Shamika develops a questionnaire with open-ended questions designed to inform her of the types of research that individuals have conducted who were using the database as well as their perceptions of the database. She asks a couple of probing questions because she wants something more than, "This is awesome!" Shamika distributes her questionnaires to the two professors who have brought their classes to the library for training and asks them to distribute them in class. Students will be asked to include their names and contact information if they wish to be contacted for further information.

Shamika sets up a list of criteria that she will be looking for as she reviews the questionnaires. She develops a matrix where she will code her data and enter the results. When the questionnaires are returned to Shamika, she enters the results in the matrix and notes patterns and similarities. She contacts the students and professors that she has identified as providing the most powerful information and asks to meet with them individually for a follow-up interview. Shamika asks more in-depth questions during her in-depth interviews and will present a final report to the director based on her most powerful impact statements. Shamika initially randomized her sample by distributing the questionnaires to both classes. She concluded with a purposeful random sample by exploring the results of her questionnaire and determining the individuals who would best fit for her data.

Sampling Politically Important Cases

The case study researcher must be aware of and sensitive to political influences that are involved in a case study. During an election year, political acumen is extremely important. Todd met Representative Gates once at a fundraiser. Todd chatted with Gates briefly about adult literacy. Todd has just learned that Gates is running for senator. Todd is aware that a branch library located in Representative Gates's district has just completed an adult literacy program that they perceived as being highly effective. Todd immediately contacts the branch manager and asks her to complete a series of interviews and to do a cross-analysis and synthesize the results to document the effectiveness of this program. Todd will collect these data and will write a letter to Representative Gates including specific high-impact statements from the case study reports and will request funding for another funding cycle.

Convenience Sampling

Convenience sampling is by far the most familiar and the most often used sampling strategy. These cases are easily accessible and inexpensive. The main problem with convenience sampling is that there are typically no controls and they have little reliability. Convenience sampling is neither purposeful nor strategic. Additionally, there may be significant privacy issues involved with convenience sampling. While the researcher should engage the reader, case studies are not just creative stories.

Sarah has been assigned a case study to write for her library management class. Sarah immediately thinks about her library director, Elmer Hamilton. Elmer is the strangest creature on the face of the earth, and Sarah decides that the entire class and even the professor will be well entertained with her tales about Elmer. She does not think about a strategy for her case study. She does not need any documents. Elmer's stories will be sufficient without any other documentation. She writes her tales using expressive adjectives. She describes Elmer's scummy friends from the city hall that come to visit every day. She describes Elmer's lack of fashion skills including the totally unfashionable tie that he wears every day that has an accumulation of every spaghetti dinner that he has ever eaten at the Moose Lodge.

Sarah is astounded when she receives an email from her professor reminding her of her earlier admonition against using convenience sampling. The professor's note further chastises her for ignoring all canons of scientific research. Sarah has not included the context for her case study, a definition of the problem other than her perception that Mr. Hamilton is weird with no research questions, hypotheses, evidences of a conceptual framework, investigations, assertions, or triangulation. Her data cannot be generalized.

Sampling choices for multiple case studies should be representative of the primary case. Purposeful sampling indicates an understanding of the problem that is being studied as well as laying the groundwork for generalizability. The case study researcher will typically select cases that offer as many perspectives as possible on the problem, process, program, or activity. If the focus is on an individual or an individual program as an exemplary case, the researcher will need to establish criteria for identifying the case. When a researcher cannot gain access to the individual or program that is most desirable, it may be that this researcher must settle for a similar case that is accessible.

BOUNDING THE CASE

Stake (1995) defined a case as a bounded system. Using the system metaphor, cases are envisioned as holistic entities with individual parts that function in their system or environment. When we speak of a bounded case, we are talking about the outline or boundaries of the system that we are discussing or evaluating (Johnson & Christensen, 2008). The purpose of using a case study in program evaluation is to determine how the system operates in a heuristic manner. The case study researcher wants to see how the parts come together and are synergized.

CASE STUDY PROTOCOL

Case study research does not follow a formal protocol like many other research methods. Even though case study research does not follow a set protocol, a researcher will develop a customized protocol to use with each individual case and should communicate this protocol to the individuals involved in the research. However, the case study researcher will soon find that establishing boundaries in the form of a case study protocol will facilitate the flow of information and data collection procedures.

Having a protocol will keep the study on target and help to provide more reliable results. Yin (2009) recommends including an overview of the case study project, field procedures, case study questions, and a guide for the case study report in a case study protocol.

An overview of the case study project covers the background information about the project, substantive issues, and relevant readings or a literature review on the topic. The overview will include the purpose and the people involved in conducting and sponsoring the project.

Field procedures will not be totally controlled in a case study as with an experimental design. The nature of case studies is naturalistic. Even though the environment should be natural and relaxed, the case study researcher needs to sufficiently plan for the unexpected. It is best to make the field procedures as operational as possible (Yin, 2009). Interview questions and techniques should be the same among specific groups but may vary with different groups. For example, the interview questions for all students should be the same but the questions for administrators would be different than the ones that you will ask students; nevertheless, the questions for all of the administrators would be the same. In an experimental treatment, everyone would receive the same treatment regardless of age, position, or other criteria. Field procedures should include a plan for gaining access to key interviewees.

Case study questions should be substantive and specific. The questions will be ones that the client and stakeholders want to answer in the course of the study and not the actual survey questions that may be used for participants. The researcher along with the client and stakeholders should identify a list of possible documents, interviewees, or observations for each question. The evaluation questions become the structural or conceptual framework.

The basic outline of the case study report should be part of the protocol. This outline will remain flexible but generally the outline that is agreed on in the beginning stages will also be the outline for the final report.

CONTEXT OF THE CASE

Stake (1978) encouraged evaluators to focus on a program within its immediate context. Stake argued that grounding a study within a bounded case helped to construct a more comprehensive understanding of the case. Bounding the case provides a structure or framework that the researcher will follow throughout the evaluation process. This framework will guide the researcher and all of the stakeholders in the collection and evaluation of data. Bounding the case helps to provide a clear understanding of the context and limitations of the case for everyone who is involved.

Creswell (1998) identifies this bounded system as an individual, program, event, or activity that is being studied. Creswell further defines a *multi-site study* as several programs being studied and *within-site study* as a single program (p. 61). Van Dalen (1966) describes case studies as an endeavor to trace interrelationships between facts that will provide a deeper phenomenal insight.

The researcher should provide information about the physical setting as well as details about the social, historical, and economic influences that form the context of the case. The context provides a preliminary description of the setting and some preliminary information on how this context will be interpreted such as the analysis of themes and assertions. The context of the case helps to bound the case in terms of time, events, and processes. One of the first questions that we ask when someone comes to visit our facility is, "How long will you be staying?" Everyone involved in the case should have a clear picture of the time that will be allotted for interviews, observations, and other evaluative processes.

The researcher should be careful not to provide superfluous details but should provide all of the details that the reader might need to answer questions about why this person or this group may have reacted in a certain manner. If the fact that the library director is wearing a red tie is in some way connected to the observation at hand, the researcher should include that detail. However, if the red tie has no relevance to the rest of the narrative, it should be omitted. The case study researcher will make a lot of field notes initially that may or may not be included in the final report because they are not relevant.

DEFINITION OF THE PROBLEM OR DESCRIPTION OF THE CASE

The program description provides a conceptual framework for the evaluation. If we look back at our South Central case study, we will see that we do not have a clear idea about exactly what is to be evaluated. Do the stakeholders want to know if the training that the library staff was given to conduct this program was effective? Do the librarians want to know if the information literacy program was effective? Do the librarians want to compare elements of their program and its effectiveness with benchmarking institutions? Do administrators want to know how the information literacy program contributes to academic success in general?

Foreshadowing involves a global examination of the problem. The case study researcher might mention recent journal articles or books about the topical problem, institutional research, or a similar library problem at another university or in another community. For example, a case study that is investigating a library marketing plan might mention the increasing need for library marketing and recent books and articles about library marketing. This section should focus on libraries that are as similar as possible to the one that is being investigated. While this section is not an extensive literature review, it should provide a broad coverage of current materials and resources on the topic under investigation.

INVESTIGATING

According to Stake (1995), the aim of a case study researcher in presenting a problem is to provide the reader or researcher with an understanding of the problem. The case study researcher must be an astute observer of human behavior and have acumen for problem solving. Case studies are not just entertaining stories. The narrative observation is intended to provide information to substantiate a claim or problem, to instruct, inform, or motivate the reader. The researcher must be careful to report all information accurately and thoroughly and to check any details that are questionable. The investigation should seek to explore and to answer the initial research questions and should uncover all of the variables that are related to these questions.

Ary, Jacobs, and Razavieh (1996) contend that case studies lack breadth and that one case study may have little relevance to other settings. They mention the problems of subjectivity and prejudice in recording and interpreting case observations and emphasize the importance of rigorous testing and investigation to overcome these potential problems with case studies.

SUMMARY OF GUIDELINES FOR CONDUCTING A FIELD-OBSERVATION CASE STUDY

The following summary of guidelines for conducting a field-observation case study is adapted from Robert Stake's (1995) *The Art of Case Study*, pages 52 and 53. These guidelines summarize the process for doing a field-observation case study.

Anticipation

- Review what is expected at the outset in the way of a case study.
- Consider the questions, hypotheses, or issues already raised.
- Read case study literature, both methodological and exemplary.
- Look for one or more studies possibly to use as a model.
- Identify the "case." Was it prescribed, selected to represent, or merely convenient?
- Define the boundaries of the case(s) as they appear in advance.
- Anticipate key problems, events, attributes, spaces, persons, vital signs.
- Consider possible audiences for preliminary and final reportings.
- Form initial plan of action, including definition of role of observer.

First Visit

- Arrange preliminary access, negotiate plan of action, and arrange regular access.
- Write a formal agreement indicating obligations for observer and for host.
- Refine access rules with people involved regarding human subjects.
- Discuss real or potential costs to hosts, including opportunity costs.
- Discuss arrangements for maintaining confidentiality of data, sources, and reports.
- Discuss need for persons to review drafts to validate observations and descriptions.
- Discuss publicity to be given during and following the study.
- Identify information and services, if any, to be offered hosts.
- Revise action plan, observer's role, case boundaries, and issues.

Preparation for Observation

- Make preliminary observations of activities.
- Use other sites for pilot cases.
- Allocate resources to alternative spaces, persons, methods, issues, and phases.
- Identify informants and sources of particular data.
- Select or develop instruments or standardized procedures.
- Work out record-keeping system, files, tapes; coding system; protected storage.
- Rework priorities for attributes, problems, events, and audiences.

Conceptualization

- Reconsider issues or other theoretical structure to guide the data gathering.
- Learn what audience members know, what they want to come to understand.
- Sketch plans for final report and dissemination of findings.
- Identify the possible "multiple realities," different perspectives.
- Allocate attention to different viewpoints, conceptualizations.

Gather and Validate Data

- Make observations, interview, debrief informants, and gather logs, use surveys and other assessment methods.
- Keep records of inquiry arrangements and activities.
- Select vignettes, special testimonies, illustrations.
- Classify raw data; begin interpretations.
- Redefine issues, case boundaries, renegotiate arrangements with hosts, as needed.
- Gather more data, to replicate, triangulate, or validate *observations*.

Data Analysis

- Review raw data under various possible interpretations.
- Search for data patterns.
- Seek linkages between program arrangements, activities, and outcomes.
- Draw tentative conclusions, organize according to issues, and organize final report.
- Review data, gather new data, seek disconfirmation of findings.

Audience Participation in Reporting

- Describe extensively the setting within which the activity occurred.
- Consider the report as a story; look for ways in which it is complete.
- Draft reports and reproduce materials for audience use.
- Try them out on representative members of audience groups.
- Discern typicality and relevance of situation for generalization.
- Revise and disseminate reports and materials.
- Talk to people to determine reactions and to gain new insights.

The researcher should consider the fiscal and human resources that will be needed for the evaluation, any training that will be required, special software or technologies that may be needed, and the political context of the organization. We will discuss these items more thoroughly in the next chapters.

CASE APPLICATION

I mentioned some of my concerns about bounding the study in the previous chapter. I met with Drs. Walters and Porter at the end of my first frustrating day. Dr. Porter graciously greeted me as I entered her office with the comment, "I'm sure that you must have lots of questions after your first day here." Wow, was that an understatement! She informed me that she had scheduled a meeting at 5:00 p.m. with the library committee and Dr. Walters. This meeting was not on my agenda but I felt more comfortable with the idea of meeting with these other stakeholders in the beginning. She told me that she would bring the contract with her to that meeting for me to sign.

I asked her some of my questions about the availability of data and key individuals and she assured me that I would have complete access to anyone and any information that I would need to successfully complete my report. I asked her some brief questions about ethics and protocol and decided that I would wait until I met with the library committee and Dr. Walters to ask some more specific questions that would help me to bound the study and to determine the approach that I would take. What are some questions that I should ask Dr. Walters and the library committee when I meet with them?

APPLICATION QUESTIONS AND EXERCISES

1. After reviewing the South Central case study, I have several questions that need to be answered. How would you go about finding the answers to these questions after reading this chapter?
   a. How old is the information literacy program? It was apparently recently added to the curriculum but is it built on a previous program?
   b. Have there been any previous efforts to evaluate the information literacy program? If so, by whom? When?
   c. What were the findings?
   d. How was the program revised as the result of these findings?
   e. Why does the administration want the program evaluated now?
2. I have been told that the information literacy program is controversial because it is a three-credit-hour course.
   a. Are there other reasons that it is controversial?
   b. Who are the advocates for the course? Who are the opponents?
   c. What decisions will be made as a result of the evaluation?
3. I have been told that the course will be dropped.
   a. Will the library continue to offer this course as a noncredit course?
   b. Will this affect library staffing in any way?
4. How broadly does the curriculum committee sample opinions of administrators, faculty, and students?
5. To what extent have those groups had the opportunity to provide input?
6. Is there any documentation of their input?

7. Do they feel that their input was valued?
8. Were any changes made as a result of their comments?
9. How well is the South Central library integrated with other departments?
10. Is the relationship congenial? Competitive?
11. What are the costs of the information literacy program (dollars, time)?
12. Are there any problems with continued university support to provide budget and staffing for this program?
13. What resources are available to conduct the evaluation?
14. Will South Central administrators and library faculty be available to assist with gathering data, scheduling interviews, program observation, and preparing the report?
15. What training will be necessary?
16. What access will I have to collect the data that I need?
17. What are the campus IRB policies regarding interviews and observations?
18. What policies or protocol do I need to be aware of in preparing and distributing the report?
19. Are there any other materials that might give me a better view of the program?
20. What are the activities and major components?
21. What methods are used?
22. How do these activities and methods link to the goals and objectives of the program?

At this point, I do not know anything about the goals and objectives or the conceptual framework.

23. What do the faculty and instructional design experts on campus see as the theory or model for the program?
24. How do they think the program activities and methods lead to program success?
25. Have they modeled the program on other programs with which they are familiar? If so, what programs?
26. What successes have these programs demonstrated?
27. What literature has been cited in the program description to provide evidence for why the model should work?
28. What is the time frame for this evaluation? What will be the budget?

MAJOR CHAPTER THEMES

Learning the needs and perceptions of the evaluation from different potential audiences is the first step in analyzing the evaluation context. Developing a program description is a crucial step in setting appropriate boundaries for your study. The conceptual framework or description of the study includes goals and objectives, activities, and stakeholder characteristics.

Reviewing the program theory helps the program evaluator to formulate appropriate questions. Describing the program involves reviewing current literature, institutional documentation, interviews, and observations. Considering program resources such as budget and staff time are a critical element if the program evaluator is to be perceived as being sensitive to the needs of the political climate.

CHAPTER EVALUATION STANDARDS

Review the Joint Committee on Standards for Educational Evaluation (1994) in Appendix A. Describe the standards that are relevant to this chapter.

REFERENCES

Ary, D., Jacobs, L., & Razavieh, A. *Introduction to Research in Education*. 5th ed. Ft. Worth: Harcourt Brace, 1996.

Creswell, J. *Qualitative Inquiry and Research Design: Choosing Among Five Traditions*. Thousand Oaks, CA: Sage, 1998.

Denzin, N. *Interpretive Biography*. Qualitative Research Methods, 17. Thousand Oaks, CA: Sage, 1989.

Fitzpatrick, J., Sanders, J., & Worthen, B. *Program Evaluation Alternative Approaches and Practical Guidelines*, 3rd ed. Boston: Allyn & Bacon, 2004.

Johnson, B., & Christensen, L. *Educational Research: Quantitative, Qualitative, and Mixed Approaches*, 3rd ed. Thousand Oaks, CA: Sage, 2008.

Kanter, R. *The Change Masters*. New York: Free Press, 1983.

Patton, M. *Qualitative Evaluation Methods*, 2nd ed. Thousand Oaks, CA: Sage, 1990.

Peters, T., & Waterman, R. *In Search of Excellence: Lessons from America's Best-Run Companies*. New York: Harper & Row, 1984.

Stake, R. *The Art of Case Study Research*. Thousand Oaks, CA: Sage, 1995.

Stake, R. *The Case Study Method in Social Inquiry*. Thousand Oaks, CA: Sage, 1978.

Van Dalen, D. *Understanding Educational Research*. New York: McGraw-Hill, 1966.

Yin, R. *Case Study Research: Design and methods*. 4th ed. Thousand Oaks, CA: Sage, 2009.

6

Planning Questions and Criteria

FOCUS QUESTIONS

How does the program evaluator develop good questions?
Should the program evaluator develop all of the questions?
What constitutes good evaluation questions and criteria?
Who should be involved in identifying and selecting appropriate questions?

QUESTION DEVELOPMENT

Evaluation questions provide a focus and standardization for the evaluation. Developing appropriate questions is not a task that can be accomplished in a vacuum. The program evaluator must involve the stakeholders in the question development process to develop questions that identify the criteria or standards that are to be judged and to win their confidence.

The case study method is usually considered to be most appropriate for answering "who" and "why" questions. Yin (2009) recommends developing questions in three stages: First, review the literature and develop appropriate questions based on the literature and the key issues in the case. Second, examine closely or dissect a few key studies in your area of interest. Identify the questions in those studies and whether they indicate areas of further research. Third, examine peripheral studies on your topic that may provide potential questions or concerns. The studies that you examine should have similar characteristics and demographics to your proposed study.

Cronbach (1982) labeled the question selection process using the terms *divergent* and *convergent*. The divergent phase involves brainstorming a long list of possible questions and concerns from all of the stakeholders. The stakeholders would include a representative sample from all of the following groups: policymakers, administrators, practitioners, clients, and students. After the stakeholders are identified, they should be interviewed briefly to determine what they would like to know about the evaluation.

During this divergent process the stakeholders should share their questions and concerns, their perception of the program, and what they think the program is designed to accomplish.

It is important to encourage stakeholders to indicate how they would like to change or "grow" the program. Cousins and Earl (1995) encourage evaluators to involve stakeholders during every phase because the more they are involved, the more likely they are to use the results and to have a better understanding of the program. Involving stakeholders improves the validity of the overall evaluation.

The evaluator may serve to educate the stakeholders on program theory, current literature in the field, expert opinion, and professional standards, checklists, guidelines, instruments, or criteria used elsewhere during the interview. Generally, during the divergent phase, the primary role of the evaluator is to listen and to volunteer expert knowledge when it is requested. The evaluator may establish a context by saying something like, "As you know, I have been asked to evaluate your information literacy program. I would like for the information that I collect to be useful to you and other (students, administrators, and library staff) on campus. What are your perceptions of the program? What questions or concerns do you have about the program that you would like to see addressed in this evaluation? What are the major changes that you have seen occur as a result of this program? How do you think the program activities lead to these outcomes? What activities do you see as being most critical to the success of the program? What aspects of the program would you like to see changed?"

If a stakeholder does not address something that you think should be addressed, you might ask a follow-up question such as, "Do you have any questions about ___? What would you like to know?" Grounding the evaluation in the concerns of key people helps the evaluator to ensure that the evaluation will be useful and responsive to all constituents (Fitzpatrick, Sanders, & Worthen, 2004).

During the divergent phase of program development, it is important to consider the conceptual framework as well as the evaluation approach or design. For example, the objectives-oriented approach would lead the evaluator to develop questions relating to the goals and objectives. Questions such as, "Have the goals and objectives of the program been met?" would be common using this approach. If you are using the management-oriented approach, you would ask questions to provide information regarding the inputs and outputs of the program and questions that would enable the decision makers on campus to decide whether or not to continue the program.

If you follow the consumer-oriented model, you will develop extensive checklists and sets of criteria to determine if the individuals that are being served by the program are satisfied with the results. The expert-oriented approach would lead you down the path of professional standards and professional literature that reflect the values and opinions of experts in the field. The participant-oriented approach would encourage a more complex or holistic evaluation strategy in which representative stakeholders at all levels participate in developing questions and at all other stages of the evaluations. This approach would include elements of the other approaches. Goals and objectives, standards, checklists, professional literature, expert opinion, and internal documents and policies would serve as useful instruments in question development.

Professional standards are helpful in the question development phase because they codify acceptable practice. Since professional standards are determined by field experts, these standards and questions based on professional standards ensure a valid and reliable evaluation. Professional standards provide a necessary element in the question formation phase; they should not be the sole gauge of program success. Internal stakeholders should play an integral role in this process.

The convergent phase involves establishing a list of criteria for establishing a critical list of questions. This process will involve rating questions to determine the most important questions, consolidating some items, and filling in gaps. The stakeholders are involved with rating and refining the questions. Generally, the questions will fit into needs assessment or context, process and mentoring, and outcomes. If a decision-making element is included, there may be questions about the budget and other resources.

Cronbach (1982) proposed six criteria for determining which proposed evaluation questions should be investigated. These criteria should be developed based on the individuals who will use the information, the type of information that are being requested, and the feasibility of answering this question, given available financial and human resources, time, methods, and technology.

Cronbach (1982) recommends placing the proposed questions in a matrix using these criteria and then redistributing them to a group of stakeholders. The absolute standards or "must" statements are the most logical list of criteria to include in this matrix.

Evaluators should desist from including biased questions. Evaluation standards may be either relative or absolute depending on the stage of the program. Relative standards can be tentative standards that are formed in the early or formative stages of the evaluation. Relative standards can also be standards that are specific to an institution or group. Absolute standards are professional standards or accreditation standards that are typically stated as "must" statements.

If the evaluation is summative, the questions should be comprehensive and should provide criteria for judging program success. Professional standards may be used but should not be the only standards for judging the program. Institutional strategic plans are helpful in developing formative questions. It is also good to compare institutional goals and objectives when developing questions based on professional standards. Comparing institutional standards and professional standards for benchmarking institutions will be helpful. Developing questions based on these documents will ensure that the data that are collected are relevant and useful in the final analysis. The questions developed within the context of the evaluation are always preeminent. The evaluator will need to remain flexible throughout the process to follow up on questions that are not complete and to include new material that surfaces in the evaluation process.

FOCUSING THE EVALUATION

Even though evaluations should be flexible, an evaluator and the stakeholders should have a clear plan. Selecting the evaluation questions, criteria, and standards helps to focus the evaluation. The information that has been covered in previous chapters about evaluating the proposal, analyzing the context, and bounding the study are all elements that bring focus.

COLLECTING INFORMATION

The next important step after determining the questions that need to be answered is what information will be needed to answer these questions. That information will get back to your conceptual framework. Researchers must also determine where that information may be obtained. You will begin to make a list of resources for answering the particular questions that you have developed at this point.

Instrumentation

Instrumentation deals with designing an effective instrument that adheres to the constructs of validity, reliability and minimizes researcher bias within a descriptive-contextual setting. The instrumentation process will include developing surveys, interview questions, lists of institutional documents that you will collect, and other materials that you will collect and analyze as a part of your evaluation. All of these materials will be directly related to the questions that you plan to answer as a researcher and will fit in to your conceptual framework.

RESEARCH QUESTIONS AND CONCEPTUAL ORGANIZERS

Some case study researchers, particularly for instrumental or instructive case studies, like to provide research questions to guide the process and to engage the reader. Parlett and Hamilton (1976) call this technique "progressive focusing." Stake (1995) states that "good research questions are especially important for case studies because case and context are infinitely complex and the phenomena are fluid and elusive" (p. 33). Good research questions help to ground the researcher's observations in areas that are most relevant.

Some case study researchers produce a list of issues or problem statements to guide the reader. Information questions may be included to suggest the need for additional information. For example, the researcher may report an incident and ask the question, "What is the library's policy on this issue?" These questions may be included in the preliminary report and replaced with more complete information in the final report.

Evaluative questions may be included to determine the value of certain programs. For example, a librarian may mention the library's information literacy program. The researcher might insert the question, "How effective is the information literacy program?" In the final report, the researcher might insert survey data or some form of outcomes assessment that measures the effectiveness of the information literacy program.

Since instrumental case studies deal with a specific problem or issue, it behooves case study researchers to substantiate their findings with specific data. Patton (1990) cites a number of government studies that are classic impact studies demonstrating the synthesis of direct fieldwork, project documents, interviews, and observations to draw policy-relevant conclusions from individual project case studies.

Research questions do not have to be hypotheses statements for case studies. They may serve as hypotheses, but the main purpose is to conceptualize the framework for the study.

Peshkin (1993) recommends re-titling the case study several times in the process of writing it to gain different perspectives. The list of issues and research questions will change each time the title changes. This technique helps the researcher to maintain a nonbiased perspective and to construct an objective framework for the reader.

CASE APPLICATION

When I met with the library committee and with Dr. Walters I asked a number of questions that would help me in forming my criteria for the study. I gave them the URLs for the Association of College and Research Libraries Information Literature Competency Standards and the Joint Committee on Standards for Educational Evaluation (1994). I asked them to review these documents and then asked Dr. Porter to set up another meeting with this committee after they had reviewed these documents to develop the questions for the study.

I was concerned that the librarians who taught the information literacy course had not been invited to this meeting. I thought they should have been some of the main stakeholders. I requested that the librarians that had taught the information literacy course be invited to the next meeting.

I thought that it would be good to invite the director of institutional research to the next meeting. I wanted to see how the library's information literacy course fit into the university strategic plan. I thought that it would be good for the library committee to be apprised of linkages with the university strategic plan and the information literacy course. I also requested that the dean of students be invited to the next meeting to share her findings from the retention study that she had conducted with students with learning disabilities. All of these individuals are key players and their reports and data will make a huge difference in the perception of the information literacy program on campus. All of these individuals will help me to address the key concerns and issues with the information literacy program and will help me to ground the study in current research and in the university curricular and political structures.

The library committee includes one faculty member who is enthusiastic about the information literacy program. Another faculty member is new and has been recently appointed to the library committee. She does not seem to have much familiarity with the program. Another faculty member is quite vocal in his opposition. He remembers a critical thinking course that was added to the curriculum several years ago that "was just fluff" and he equates the information literacy program to this critical thinking course. Two members did not attend the meeting. The other two members who were present answered direct questions but were not forthcoming. One of them came in with the faculty member who opposed the program, sat next to him and appeared to be agreeing nonverbally with his assertions against the program.

Dr. Walters does not seem overly enthusiastic about the program. She sat next to Dr. Porter and they were chatting and passing notes about a curriculum meeting the following day. For the most part, Dr. Walters has been noncommittal. She seems supportive of the program when she is around other librarians but I cannot seem to read her within the context of the larger organization. The only thing that is obvious to me at this point is that this case study will have many challenges and that it has been and will continue to be a difficult thing to make a strong case for the information literacy program as a for-credit course.

Drs. Porter and Walters agreed to schedule another meeting and to ask the other individuals that I had mentioned to attend the next meeting. Dr. Porter congratulated me on being selected to do the evaluation and presented me with a contract. We briefly discussed a timeline and the budget. I am not clear about some of the terms of the contract but I am

(continued)

sure that everything will be all right. These are all professional people. I signed the contract feeling confident that I could facilitate this evaluation and that the key stakeholders would fulfill their various roles to make this a useful evaluation.

Below are some of the questions that I am considering before the next meeting. What are some things that I should have done differently?

APPLICATION QUESTIONS AND EXERCISES

1. Using the South Central case, what individuals would you involve in designing the questions for evaluating this program?
2. What standards would you consult in the question design phase?
3. Should benchmarking institutions be consulted about similar programs and the standards or criteria that they have used when developing the questions for South Central?
4. What literature or professional experts might you consult during the divergent phase of question development at South Central?

MAJOR CHAPTER THEMES

This chapter questions the evaluation focus. Summative evaluations will specify the program standards and criteria. These questions provide a guide for data collection. The questions and criteria indicate the characteristics of the program that are critical to the program's success. The standards that are developed in the question development phase indicate the satisfactory level of program performance.

All key stakeholders are involved in the divergent phase of question development and in the question refinement process. The evaluator may consider evaluation models, literature, professional standards, field experts, and benchmarking institutions in the question development phase.

The convergent phase involves narrowing down the questions by establishing a list of criteria and using ratings to determine the most essential questions. Stakeholders should be involved in this process as well as the divergent phase.

CHAPTER EVALUATION STANDARDS

Review the Joint Committee on Standards for Educational Evaluation (1994) in Appendix A. Describe the standards that are relevant to this chapter.

REFERENCES

Cousins, J., & Earl, L. *Participatory Evaluation in Education: Studies in Evaluation Use and Organizational Learning*. London: Farmer, 1995.

Cronbach, L. *Designing Evaluations of Educational and Social Programs*. San Francisco: Jossey-Bass, 1982.

Fitzpatrick, J., Sanders, J., & Worthen, B. *Program Evaluation Alternative Approaches and Practical Guidelines*, 3rd ed. Boston: Allyn & Bacon, 2004.

Parlett, M., & Hamilton, D. Evaluation as Illumination: A New Approach to the Study of Innovative Programs. In G. V. Glass (Ed.), *Evaluation studies review annual* (Vol. 1). Beverly Hills, CA: Sage, 1976.

Patton, M. *Qualitative Evaluation Methods*, 2nd ed. Thousand Oaks, CA: Sage, 1990.

Peshkin, A. The Goodness of Qualitative Research. *Educational Researcher, 22* (1993): 23–29.

Stake, R. *The Art of Case Study Research*. Thousand Oaks, CA: Sage, 1995.

Yin, R. *Case Study Research: Design and Methods*. 4th ed. Thousand Oaks, CA: Sage, 2009.

7

Identifying Design and
Data Collection Methods

FOCUS QUESTIONS

What are some activities that should be considered in planning any evaluation?
What should the evaluation plan specify?
What is the role of the stakeholders in developing the plan?
What resources should be considered when developing evaluation budgets?
Discuss the reasons for developing an evaluation contract.

THE EVALUATION PLAN

After you have set appropriate boundaries and developed a focus for the evaluation, you then need to develop an evaluation plan. The evaluation plan controls the process for information collection, organization, analysis, and reporting. A final implementation or administration step could be added.

The evaluation plan or design gives the stakeholders a clear picture of the purpose and role of the evaluation. The plan should define whether the evaluation will be formative or summative. A formative evaluation is an informal evaluation in which instruments are developed and pilot tested. The intent is to refine the instruments and to improve the program before the summative evaluation. The summative evaluation will be the formal evaluation in which the instruments will be used to assess the outcomes and efficacy of the program.

The plan should identify the focus of the evaluation, whether the evaluation will be comparative or descriptive, and the orientation that the stakeholders have chosen. A comparative evaluation will compare one program to one or more similar programs for benchmarking institutions. A descriptive evaluation will provide a thick, complete description of one program. The orientation might include any of the six styles that were discussed in previous chapters: decision-oriented, objectives-oriented, management-oriented, consumer-oriented, expertise-oriented, or participant-oriented.

Designs dictate the organization or structure for collecting data and may be either causal or descriptive. If the program is at the pilot state, the design and evaluation will be descriptive. If the program has moved beyond the formative stage and the stakeholders are requesting a summative evaluation activity, then a causal design measuring actual performance would be more appropriate.

Descriptive designs would be used for case studies, and these include some of the following: *time-series design, cross-sectional design, case study,* or *thick description.* The design that the evaluator selects depends on whether the research question(s) indicate a study that will show a trend, illustrate a process, convey status, or describe and analyze a program, process, or procedure. It is common to incorporate several designs to address all of the research questions or to ensure reliability and validity. The stakeholders should review the questions with the evaluator to make sure that the proposed research design(s) adequately cover the entire spectrum of questions.

IDENTIFYING SOURCES OF INFORMATION

Six entities are used to gather data; these include talking with individuals who

1. have a knowledge of the nature of the case;
2. know its historical background;
3. know the physical setting;
4. are aware of other contexts, including economic, political, legal, and aesthetic;
5. know other cases through which this case is recognized; and
6. are very aware of other informants from outside who may be familiar with the program. (Stake, 1995)

Examining each question, the evaluator and the stakeholders should jointly determine appropriate sources of information or data for each question.

Both primary and secondary resources should be considered in the process of identifying appropriate sources. Use existing data such as previous evaluation reports, status reports, data and statistics gathered for other reports, and other internal data that may be appropriate. Public documents and databases are sometimes useful. It is important to guard against what Patton (1986) refers to as a Type III error: gathering impressive data that answer the wrong question.

Some sources for gathering data or information include the following:

• Program recipients or participants (i.e., students, librarians, professors)
• Program administrators (librarians, professors, administrators)
• Policymakers (board members)
• Funding agencies
• Field experts
• Existing data and documents
• Direct observation

METHODS FOR COLLECTING DATA

Worthen, Borg, and White (1993) have provided a useful classification scheme for prompting evaluators in planning methods of data collection. This scheme could easily be developed into a rubric for data collection. The steps include data collected from individuals, personal products such as tests, observations, existing information such as public documents and personal files, and technological data such as audio or video tapes.

After the list of data has been constructed, the stakeholders and the evaluator should review the list for relevance, utility, availability, and soundness. They should jointly consider the costs for obtaining data, time and scheduling constraints, reliability and validity, legal and ethical issues, and the relevance of the data to the final evaluation. If the evaluator will involve other individuals in collecting data, training sessions should be planned.

COLLECTING INFORMATION

Time constraints generally call for using a representative sample of the population. Sampling can be useful and valid if a group is chosen that is representative of the whole. Sampling techniques are described in Chapter 5. It is best to work with the director of institutional research or someone else with a statistics background on your campus to help you to determine a representative sample.

The conditions under which the data will be collected should be determined as nearly as possible at the outset. The program design should specify who will collect various data, trainings, data checks, the setting in which data will be collected, equipment and material needs, and ethical issues.

A timeline should be developed in consensus with the evaluator and the stakeholders. All parties should have a clear idea about when information will be needed and when it can reasonably be delivered.

ORGANIZING, ANALYZING, AND INTERPRETING INFORMATION

Planning how the data will be organized, analyzed, and interpreted is an important part of the design process. Design processes should be planned for coding, organizing, storing, manipulating, and retrieving the information that is gathered. The evaluator and the stakeholders should examine each question and identify the methods that will be used for analyzing the data and the results for that question.

Four tests are commonly used as a standard of quality for qualitative reliability. These four tests are construct validity, internal validity, external validity, and reliability (Kidder & Judd, 1986, pp. 26–29). Yin (2009) recommends breaking each of these steps down using the following tactics. The first is using multiple sources of evidence to establish a chain of evidence to construct validity. He further recommends pattern matching and explanation building to provide internal validity and to address rival explanations. Logic models are also helpful in this process. Theory in single-case studies and replication logic in multiple-case studies helps to establish external validity. Developing a case study database and carefully following case study protocol helps to make an evaluation more reliable (Yin, 2009, p. 41).

REPORTING THE RESULTS

The evaluator and the stakeholders should have a list of questions for which data should be obtained for the final report. Some reports may include documentation of meetings, presentations, and informal discussions. Other reports may include statistical or technical data. Brinkeroff et al. (1983) recommend designing a reporting matrix for each question that will identify the audience, the content to be included, the reporting format, the date of the report, and the context in which the report will be presented.

The case study researcher may take on any number of roles in presenting a case study. Stake (1995) identifies seven roles that are prominent among case study researchers. A consultant will apply these roles within the library context.

The Case Study Researcher as Teacher

Any research should inform or educate the reader. One of the most important roles of the case study researcher in the library science field is to educate the reader concerning how to conduct a study, in this book, a case study in a particular setting. This allows the teacher researcher to translate that meaning by using common themes, ethical issues, morals, and other behavioral analysis.

The Case Study Researcher as Advocate and Evaluator

The case study researcher as advocate uses case study findings to accommodate theoretical discourse to facilitate change. The case study researcher as evaluator is a more detailed role.

Evaluation of individual or program strengths or weaknesses is perhaps one of the most complex roles that a case study researcher assumes due to the complexities of individual and organizational behavior. It is important for the researcher clearly and accurately to describe contexts, consider multiple viewpoints, and triangulate findings using multiple measures and the literature. Any kind of program evaluation works best when all of the individuals involved are aware of the evaluation measures to be used from the beginning of the program or study.

The Case Study Researcher as Biographer

Since many case studies revolve around a person, the case study researcher is often a biographer. As a biographer, Stake (1995) cautions against reducing the individual to a caricature. The researcher must thoroughly examine the context within which the individual is being studied and develop a thematic network to examine the appropriate phase of the person's life for the purpose of the case study. The researcher does not want to include irrelevant, distracting details such as the type of automobiles the librarians drive. On the other hand, the researcher does not want to neglect to include even the most minor detail that might strengthen the case, such as the fact that the person seems to be unnecessarily sensitive to even simple suggestions.

The Case Study Researcher as Interpreter

The role of the researcher as interpreter is central to the case study research process. Stake (1995) points out that researchers must make choices about their role in the interpretative process. They must make decisions at the outset about how much or if they should participate personally in the case or to pose as an expert, whether to be a neutral observer or critical analyst, and whether to narrate the case as a story or make it more clinical in nature. The researcher is charged with the task of interpreting findings to the person who did the hiring, stakeholders, and the readers of the report. The researcher presents the facts and generalizes them to make sense of a problem and to provide an interpretation of the problem within the proper context.

The Case Study Researcher as Constructivist

Stake (1995) makes the point that qualitative researchers practice the belief that knowledge is not just discovered but is rather constructed. Our worlds are formed by perceptions of reality—our perception of reality and the perceptions of others of that same reality. The case study researcher seeks to blend or construct all of these realities and to help the reader to make sense of the situation or individual as a whole as a part of all of these realities. A constructivist case study researcher provides sufficient raw material to allow the reader to interpret people and events in a thorough and logical manner.

The Case Study Researcher as Relativist

A researcher's views are relevant to his or her experience or involvement in the case. The reader's interpretation of the case is relevant to his or her experiences, circumstances surrounding the case, and the reader's involvement with the researcher or the individual in the case. It is usually easy to tell when reading college students' case studies how they are related to the subject. When they write about that cruel, incompetent library director, they are typically not writing about themselves. It is important to avoid biases at all levels and to strive to create a view that will allow the reader to consider the case objectively.

Fitzpatrick, Sanders, and Worthen (2004) recommend using worksheets to specify the information required, report design(s), source(s), method(s), information-collection arrangements, analysis procedures, and interpretation procedures. These may include standards or benchmarking and reporting procedures.

THE MANAGEMENT PLAN

Evaluations are costly in terms of human and fiscal resources. Many evaluators recommend developing a Program Evaluation and Review Technique (PERT) or Gantt chart to document and account for the resources that will be used in an evaluation. PERT charts are generally too time-consuming and cumbersome for most projects. Gantt charts include a list of tasks on the vertical axis and a timeline on the horizontal axis. Many examples of both PERT and Gantt charts can be found online and in program evaluation textbooks.

EVALUATION BUDGETING

The evaluation budget, like all aspects of the design process, should be planned jointly with the evaluator and the stakeholders to prevent any misunderstandings. An evaluation budget should typically include the following ten categories (Sanders, 1983).

1. Evaluation staff salary and benefits: Personnel costs are the highest proportion of any budget. University employees may "volunteer" their time for the project but they are taking time

away from their normal duties. This means that the time that they spend on the evaluation project should be factored into the cost of the evaluation. To figure this amount, you can take their annual salary, divide this by 12 if they are on a twelve-month contract, divide this number by 20 working days, and finally divide this number by 8. You can then multiply your final number by the number of hours this person will spend on the project. Similarly, you can figure the amount that is spent on benefits for this employee. If a new employee is hired solely to work on the evaluation, that employee's total salary and benefits would be entered.

2. Consultants: Consultants are sometimes needed to provide an outside perspective or to provide expertise that is not available onsite. Consultants may charge an hourly or daily rate and sometimes charge for other expenses such as travel and meals. It is important to clarify these items with the consultant before signing a contract.

3. Travel and per diem for staff and consultants: These items will generally be dictated by state or university policy and should be clearly identified in the budget and in all contracts.

4. Communication (postage, telephone calls): Many of these items may be fixed costs. Any variable costs should be included in the budget.

5. Printing and binding: These costs may include additional costs for webpage design if the data and final report are to be placed on the Web.

6. Data processing: New software or any other costs associated with data processing such as a computer server or outsourcing data for processing.

7. Printed materials: This includes the costs for books, surveys, or other printed materials.

8. Supplies and equipment: This category includes any supplies and equipment that are purchased for the project.

9. Subcontracts: This category may include legal services, accounting, test development, and any special service contracts.

10. Overhead (facilities, utilities): You should not include fixed costs, just costs associated with the project.

CONTRACTS

Once everyone has agreed on the project budget, contracts should be issued for the evaluator and the subcontractors. The Joint Committee (1984, p. 87) suggest guidelines for the agreement. Stufflebeam (2000) offers some helpful advice about avoiding the pitfalls of poorly drafted contracts. The evaluator and the subcontractors should also sign an ethical agreement outlining the ethics and standards relating to the project. Two documents that should be consulted in this process are the *Guiding Principles* and the *Program Evaluation Standards*. These documents may be examined and downloaded at www.eval.org. The evaluator should also consult with university administrators about Internal Review Board policies and procedures.

THE PROGRAM EVALUATION STANDARDS:
DESIGNING EVALUATIONS

The Joint Committee is a coalition of major professional associations concerned with the quality of evaluation. The Joint Committee has published three sets of standards for evaluations that are widely recognized. The Personnel Evaluation Standards were published in 1988, the *Program Evaluation Standards* (2nd edition) were published in 1994 by Sage Publications, and the Student Evaluations Standards were published in 2003.

The Joint Committee is accredited by the American National Standards Institute (ANSI). Standards approved by ANSI become American National Standards. In addition to setting standards in evaluation, it is also involved in reviewing and updating its published standards (every five years); training policymakers, evaluators, and educators in the use of the standards; and serving as a clearinghouse on evaluation standards literature.

The *Program Evaluation Standards* is a compilation of advice from hundreds of practitioners in education and evaluation. Other documents related to evaluation functions are available. The evaluation functions covered in this series are the following:

1. Deciding Whether to Evaluate
2. Defining the Evaluation Problem
3. Designing the Evaluation
4. Collecting Information
5. Analyzing Information
6. Reporting the Evaluation
7. Budgeting the Evaluation
8. Contracting for Evaluation
9. Managing the Evaluation
10. Staffing the Evaluation

CASE APPLICATION

When I had my second meeting with the stakeholders there was a definite synergy in the room. I shared some matrices to help organize the data that I had collected and we discussed a couple of questions for each matrix. We went through the exercise of identifying the information and data that we would collect to answer each question. We listed the individuals or sources that would provide the information that was needed. It was exciting to see the group take ownership of the process. I could tell that they were beginning to feel empowered as they completed the matrices. Another thing that I noticed was that some of the people that had initially seemed distant and even antagonistic toward the information literacy program were becoming excited about it as they realized how it supported institutional goals and objectives and to review some of the institutional studies such as the one that Dr. Anderson had conducted with students with learning disabilities. I could sense a camaraderie and school pride as they talked about some of the benchmarking data that Dr. Sanders and the librarians had collected.

I decided that perhaps the best approach would be to allow them to complete the matrices and to have an opportunity to compare data among themselves. Because there were a few missing pieces that they needed to gather before they completed the matrices, I also decided to schedule another appointment with the committee the following week. They will send me a rough draft by the end of the week and I will review it and perhaps make some suggestions before I meet with them next week.

It is clear now that they believe that this case is their evaluation plan. They do not view it as an amorphous report that I will develop and that they will stick in file cabinets and forget about in a few days. This is their plan and they are taking pride in developing an evaluation plan that will be an integral part of the information literacy program and I believe will shape their views of program evaluation throughout the university.

APPLICATION QUESTIONS

1. Using the evaluation questions you developed at the end of the last chapter, develop an evaluation and management plan to address these questions. What further information do you need to do that?
2. What stakeholders should you involve in planning the evaluation design?

MAJOR CHAPTER THEMES

The evaluator should plan methods for addressing each question. The evaluator should outline possible data sources and determine the availability and feasibility of using existing data for each question. The evaluator should determine the best source (s) for obtaining original data and the availability of those sources for each question. The evaluator should identify appropriate sources and cost-effective methods for completing interviews, surveys, observations, and other data. The evaluator should determine if sampling will be used and how sampling populations will be determined.

Design procedures should be identified for conducting the project. Who will collect the data? When will the data be collected? Under what conditions? What training(s) will be necessary?

A management plan such as a PERT or Gantt chart should be developed to provide the evaluator and the stakeholders with a clear project timeline. The evaluator should plan an adequate budget in terms of human and fiscal resources for the project. The evaluator and the stakeholders should work out a contractual agreement clearly indicating the purpose(s) of the evaluation, the activities to be completed, the responsibilities for each, and the salary, per diem, and other fees agreed on by both parties.

CHAPTER EVALUATION STANDARDS

Review the Joint Committee on Standards for Educational Evaluation (1994) in Appendix A. Describe the standards that are relevant to this chapter.

REFERENCES

Brinkerhoff, R. O., Brethower, D. M., Hluckyj, T., & Nowakowski, R., Jr. *Program Evaluation: A Practitioner's Guide for Trainers and Educators*. Boston: Kluwer-Nijhoff, 1983.

Fitzpatrick, J., Sanders, J., & Worthen, B. *Program Evaluation Alternative Approaches and Practical Guidelines*, 3rd ed. Boston: Allyn & Bacon, 2004.

Kidder, L., & Judd, C. Research Methods in Social Relations, 5th ed. New York: Holt, Rinehart & Winston, 1986.

Patton, M. Q. *Utilization-focused evaluation*. 2nd ed. Beverly Hills, CA: Sage, 1986.

Sanders, J. Cost Implications of the Standards. In M. C. Alkin & L. C. Solman, (eds.). *The Cost of Evaluation*. Beverly Hills, CA: Sage, 1983.

Stake, R. *The Art of Case Study Research*. Thousand Oaks, CA: Sage, 1995.

Stufflebeam, D. L. Lessons in Contracting for Evaluations. *American Journal of Evaluation, 21* (2000): 293–314.

Worthen, B. R., Borg, W. R., & White, K. R. *Measurement and Evaluation in the Schools*. White Plains, NY: Longman, 1993.

Yin, R. K. *Case Study Research: Design and Methods, 4th ed.* Thousand Oaks, CA: Sage, 2009.

8

Establishing and Maintaining Appropriate Political, Ethical, and Interpersonal Relationships

FOCUS QUESTIONS

What procedures will you recommend for reducing interpersonal, financial, or organizational biases in the evaluation project?
Describe the ethical guidelines that you should follow in conducting evaluation studies.
What types of political influences can you anticipate causing problems in your study?
What is the political context for the evaluation?

POLITICAL DIMENSIONS IN PROGRAM PLANNING

Boleman and Deal (2008) discuss the importance of political dimensions in the organizational process. Every organization has a political structure and there are numerous political dimensions within that structure. As an evaluator you will need to function effectively within this political environment and master managerial skills to communicate effectively with administrators, develop an agenda, map the environment, manage relationships with both allies and enemies, and negotiate compromise.

Organizations have internal politics and political agendas, resources, and strategies. Sometimes different departments or individuals within organizations have different agendas or priorities from the organization as a whole. It will be your job as an evaluator to foster relationships and to establish a professional rapport with all of the constituencies within the organization where you are conducting your evaluation.

Ethical and interpersonal relationships are equally important in the evaluation process. A program evaluator should become familiar with the Joint Committee Guiding Principles and the *Program Evaluation Standards*. Additionally, a program evaluator should become familiar with internal policies and standards of conduct.

Establishing open communication is the main key to avoiding political, ethical, and interpersonal misunderstandings. Biases, ethical issues, and political pressures may also come into play in the evaluation process.

MAINTAINING GOOD COMMUNICATION

Previous chapters have discussed the importance of involving clients and stakeholders in every aspect of the evaluation process. Evaluation should be a positive learning experience for everyone involved. Too often evaluation is perceived as a threat and clients and stakeholders immediately have a negative mindset toward the evaluation activity. Try to foster a positive attitude from the beginning by informing everyone of the potential positive benefits for their department or organization. Assure clients, stakeholders, and participants that you will adhere to ethical principles and university standards.

Provide everyone who is involved with regular updates using a website or other means. Provide information about the benefits of continuous improvement in higher education in general. Find and share specific examples of positive evaluation activities or similar ones if no specific examples are available. It is important that this appears to be a more common experience than a unique one.

Continue to involve representatives from all client, stakeholder, and participant groups throughout the evaluation process. They should be involved in developing the evaluation plan, data collection, analysis, results, and interpretations. These individuals can also provide helpful advice on disseminating information to all parties involved and can provide suggestions about scheduling and timing for various evaluation activities and disseminating results. Listen to concerns, consider objections, and receive constructive criticism.

Teamwork is important throughout the evaluation process. Negotiation and compromise should be fostered and diverse viewpoints should be encouraged. If teamwork is encouraged throughout the evaluation, it will be much easier for the team to implement projects and to accomplish goals after the formal evaluation is over. Linking both short- and long-term goals to the evaluation is a part of the continuous improvement process.

Teamwork means involving everyone in all of the aspects of design and reporting and also in the actual evaluation activity. Individuals feel more empowered if they are assigned tasks such as training, testing, reporting, and analyzing data.

The Joint Committee on Standards for Educational Evaluation (1994) issued the following human interactions standard: "Evaluators should respect human dignity and worth in their interactions with other persons associated with an evaluation, so that participants are not threatened or harmed" (p. 99). Respect for people and responsibility for general and public welfare are two of the American Evaluation Association's Guiding Principles for Evaluators that are codes of behavior.

GUARDING AGAINST BIAS

We all have biases and we may be aware of our ethnic, cultural, gender, racial, age, economic, and societal biases. However, some of your team may think they are accepting of other cultures, races, or genders when in fact they are not. Awareness of our beliefs and biases is the first step in appropriately dealing with any bias issues and overcoming them. The teamwork concept helps to guard against any individual biases of the program evaluator and it should help to recognize any biases in other members of the team so they are not built into the plans. Examples of this may be the treatment of females by males or someone with a degree from an Ivy League university who ignores comments from others who have attended less-prestigious higher education institutions.

The exact antithesis of bias is when an evaluator completely accepts the beliefs and values of an organization and cannot objectively report the findings of the study. Lincoln and Guba (1981) discuss the anthropological concepts "going native" and ethnocentrism. "Going native" occurs when evaluators become so engrossed in a culture that they either consciously or unconsciously adopts their beliefs and values and refuse to present any findings that would be detrimental to the group that they are evaluating. Lincoln and Guba (1981) suggest three strategies for avoiding ethnocentricity and "going native." They suggest keeping careful reflexive logs, peer debriefing, and maintaining a consistent audit trail. Meta-evaluation, an evaluation of an evaluation, is another technique that is often used to minimize bias. It is similar to the audit trail exercise that Lincoln and Guba recommended.

Evaluators should disclose any relationships at the outset that may predispose them to bias. Ethically evaluators should disclose any relationships before a contract is signed and should not become involved in the evaluation if they feel that these relationships could in any away affect the manner in which the evaluation is conducted.

The evaluator should not profit in any way from the outcome of the evaluation. For example, if an evaluator who sells library automation software is coming to evaluate your library automation system, this person should disclose that fact. Another potential financial pitfall is if evaluators fear that they will not be paid for the evaluation if they present any negative findings.

The evaluator should disclose any previous organizational ties that may be perceived as a conflict of interest before signing a contract. If you or a friend or family member has had some negative experience with an organization in the past, this could bias your opinions of the organization.

MAINTAINING ETHICAL STANDARDS

Worthen and Sanders (1987) identify five forms of "evaluation corruptibility" that can potentially result from ethical compromises or distortions. These forms of corruptibility include conflicts of interest, unsubstantiated opinions, alleged findings that result from the evaluator's personal prejudices, and failure to honor commitments that could have been honored (p. 289).

Hatch (2002) proposed a list of ethical questions for researchers to consider in educational settings that help the researcher to avoid unethical pitfalls (p. 221). These lists are by no means exhaustive. They do provide a general sense of the ethical problems that an evaluator may face. The two ethical codes for evaluation most often used are the *Program Evaluation Standards* developed by the Joint Committee on Standards for Educational Evaluation (1994) and the Guiding Principles for Evaluators developed by the American Evaluation Association (1995).

The *Program Evaluation Standards* serve both evaluators and consumers in judging the quality of an evaluation. The Guiding Principles for Evaluators provide guidance for evaluators in their professional performance.

The *Program Evaluation Standards* include four categories: utility, feasibility, propriety, and accuracy. The third category, "propriety," addresses ethical issues such as service orientation, formal agreements, and rights of human subjects, human interactions, complete and fair assessment, disclosure of findings, conflict of interest, and fiscal responsibility. The Guiding Principles for Evaluators include five principles: systematic inquiry, competence, integrity/honesty, respect for people, and responsibilities for general and public welfare.

Previous chapters have discussed the importance of involving the client, stakeholders, and participants in every aspect of the evaluation. All of these individuals, not just the evaluator, are responsible for maintaining an ethical environment in the evaluation process.

POLITICAL PRESSURES

As noted in the beginning of this chapter, evaluators must effectively negotiate the political influences within and outside an organization. Politics becomes a negative part of the evaluation when an organization or stakeholders interject unethical practices in the evaluation process or in the manner in which the results are manipulated or reported.

Morris and Cohn (1993) conducted a survey of professional evaluators and found that nearly two-thirds of the evaluators in their study had dealt with ethical challenges. Most of these pressures or compromises involved demands from stakeholders. Some of them included pressure to alter the presentation of data; findings were suppressed or ignored by the stakeholder; evaluator discovered behavior that was illegal, unethical, and dangerous; and the evaluator was pressured to violate confidentiality. Also, findings were used to punish an employee, findings were deliberately modified by the stakeholder, stakeholder declared certain research questions off-limits, and legitimate stakeholders were omitted from the planning process.

Brikell (1978) offers some additional helpful rules of thumb for dealing with political influences (p. 98). Brickell's rules involve a remedial strategy that provides guidance for the researcher in the diagnosis of error, application of a corrective procedure, and sensitization of program personnel. These steps help the researcher and all of the individuals involved with the evaluation to recognize potential political influences that might affect the data and to take appropriate corrective measures.

CASE APPLICATION

I could not help overhearing a conversation between Drs. Porter and Walters as I walked past Dr. Walter's office to the small office that I had been given to work in the library. I really wish that I would not have heard their conversation. I had felt so confident about my progress here after our last meeting. I had spoken with Dr. Porter last Friday and she had informed me that the committee had completed the questions and seemed positive about everything. Now I could not believe my ears.

Dr. Porter had just assured Dr. Walters that the curriculum committee would not approve adding the information literacy course to the curriculum no matter what happened with the evaluation. I had always been suspicious that Dr. Walters was not fully supportive of the program but I could not understand why she would not be supportive. Just as I was trying to sort things out, Welma Pinehurst came to the door. Welma Pinehurst was the lead instructor for the information literacy course and Jason's supervisor. I greeted her and suggested that we go to the café for a cup of coffee.

I started the conversation by commenting on the wonderful comments that I had heard about the information literacy program on campus. I remarked that Dr. Walters must be very proud of the curriculum that she and her department had developed. "You would think so," Welma commented. I did not quite know how to proceed. "How long have you been here at South Central?" I asked, trying to change the subject. "Seventeen years," she responded. I could sense that Welma was dissatisfied at South Central. "I am trying to make the best of a bad situation until I retire," she added.

Welma then proceeded to tell me that she had applied for the directorship before Dr. Walters had come. Dr. Walters had been an old friend of Dr. Porter at the university where she previously worked and Dr. Porter had appointed Dr. Walters to the position even though all of the librarians and many of the university faculty wanted Welma to assume the position. She told me that her main concern at this point was for Jason and the rest of the staff that were being treated badly when they had worked so hard to implement a program that had received state and national recognition in library circles. I had not previously heard about any of this professional recognition. She continued to tell me that Jason and others had presented at state and national conferences and had submitted publications that had been accepted for publication in peer-reviewed journals.

I was beginning to get the picture. Dr. Walters felt threatened by the success of this program and by Welma Pinehurst. I had to do something to help Welma and Jason. I had to help South Central. All of the stakeholders had seemed so enthusiastic the last time that I met with them.

Just as Welma and I were finishing our coffee, Dr. Porter walked up to our table. She greeted us cordially and asked me to come by her office at 11:00.

I somehow felt like trouble was brewing with Dr. Porter as I entered her outer office. We quickly exchanged greetings. She cleared her throat in an authoritative manner and proceeded to tell me that there were some people that could no longer be included in our planning committee because they were already overcommitted and did not have time for another committee responsibility. "Dr. Sanders will no longer be able to join us and Dr. Anderson and furthermore it is not appropriate to invite the librarians. Dr. Walters can adequately represent the library without involving other librarians."

She also asked that I not use the report that Dr. Anderson had given me about the retention data with students with learning disabilities and that I not ask Dr. Sanders for information about benchmarking institutions. If I had not had my earlier conversation with Welma, I would have been completely baffled by her ultimatum. I am trying to decide how to manage the political aspects that I am suddenly faced with on this campus facilitate an effective evaluation. Is it even possible at this point? What will I need to do to bring about resolution and to get things back on track with the evaluation? I realize that I should have made some things more specific in my contract about reporting relationships and ethical agreements about the data that would be included.

APPLICATION QUESTIONS AND EXERCISES

1. Review the South Central case. Describe some of the political influences in this case. How will you involve these individuals and maintain good communication with them?
2. Describe some potential instances when an evaluator might "go native" or ethnocentric in the South Central case. How would you prevent these problems?
3. Describe some possible biases in the South Central case and how these might be dealt with or prevented.

4. What ethical standards should be applied in the South Central case? You might review the appendix documents.
5. Do you anticipate any ethical problems in the South Central case?

MAJOR CHAPTER THEMES

To encourage good communication, evaluators should inform stakeholders of the purposes of this evaluation and their role in this process. Evaluators should involve both internal and external stakeholders and should encourage different viewpoints.

Management plans as described in the previous chapter facilitate linking evaluation activities with future short- and long-term goals and involving stakeholders and participants in the evaluation. Evaluators should be aware of any biases that will affect the evaluation process and should disclose these biases to the organization.

The evaluator should become familiar with the *Program Evaluation Standards* and the Guiding Principles to adequately address all issues in the evaluation context in an ethical and professional manner. The evaluator should make every effort to deal openly and ethically with any political influences.

CHAPTER EVALUATION STANDARDS

Review the Joint Committee on Standards for Educational Evaluation (1994) in Appendix A. Describe the standards that are relevant to this chapter.

REFERENCES

American Evaluation Association. Guiding Principles for Evaluators. In W. R. Shadish, D. I. Newman, M. A. Scheirer, & C. Wye (Eds.), *Guiding Principles for Evaluators.* New Directions for Program Evaluation, 34, (1995): 19–26.

Boleman, L. G., & Deal, T. E. *Reframing Organizations: Artistry, Choice, and Leadership*, 4th ed. San Francisco: Jossey-Bass, 2008.

Brickell, H. M. The Influence of External Political Factors on the Role and Methodology of Evaluation. In T. D. Cook, M. L. Del Rosario, K. M. Hennigan, M. M. Mark, & W. M. K. Trochim (Eds.), *Evaluation Studies Review Annual* (Vol. 3). Beverly Hills, CA: Sage, 1978.

Hatch, J. *Doing Qualitative Research in Education Settings*. State University of New York Pr.: New York, 2002.

Joint Committee on Standards for Educational Evaluation. *The Program Evaluation Standards,* 2nd ed. Thousand Oaks, CA: Sage, 1994.

Lincoln, Y. S., & Guba, E. *Do Evaluators Wear Grass Skirts: "Going Native" and Ethnocentrism as Problems in Utilization*. Paper presented at the annual meeting of the Evaluation Research Society, Austin, TX, Sept. 30–Oct. 3, 1981.

Morris, L. L., & Cohn, R. Program Evaluators and Ethical Challenges: A National Survey. *Evaluation Review, 17* (1993, October): 621–642.

Worthen, B. R., & Sanders, J. R. *Educational Evaluation: Alternative Approaches and Practical Guidelines*, 2nd ed. New York: Longman, 1987.

9

Collecting, Analyzing, and Interpreting Data

FOCUS QUESTIONS

What is important in planning for collecting, analyzing, and interpreting data?
How should the results for quantitative data be analyzed and interpreted?

COLLECTING DATA

Stake (1995) observes that quantitative and qualitative methods differ most at the stage of data analysis. Qualitative researchers are involved with analysis throughout the study while quantitative researchers build their research on the statistical significance of one test or perhaps a collection of statistical data. Sometimes quantitative data may be used to demonstrate relationships.

It is not always necessary to use quantitative data in an attempt to show statistical significance. A good narrative description of the findings and a careful analysis of the data collection and coding may suffice. Using inferential statistics does not necessarily establish causality but they add another piece to the puzzle. Some data may already exist such as standardized test scores. Previous statistical comparisons may be available from other campus studies that may be appropriate to reference in connection with your study.

ANALYZING DATA

Choosing the appropriate test to apply to analyze data begins with what you are seeking to test—the data you will need to collect to provide the appropriate information. It then moves to how to analyze the data. We next cover content analysis and complementarity.

Content Analysis

Content analysis procedures are used to describe, analyze, and summarize trends and observations from field notes and the data that have been collected. Content analysis involves coding and organizing data so that they may be more effectively and efficiently presented in the final report.

Quantitative content analysis would involve coding units (words and themes). A researcher might count the number of times a key word or theme appeared in a library's annual report or meeting minutes. Electronic files may be examined for quantitative data using software. Quantitative content analysis is objective and easily documented.

The evaluator will want to select a statistical method that is designed to coordinate with the case if quantitative methods are used. Some of the following inferential statistical methods may be used depending on the case. Chi-square is a good method for examining relationships between nominal and interval data or ratios.

ANOVA and t-tests can be used for examining relationships between nominal and interval variables. Multiple regression methods might be used to explore relationships among variables or independent effects of many variables on one dependent variable.

Qualitative content analysis would provide summaries of documents. For example, the researcher might code the library meeting minutes for the year 2006. This person might note that the minutes for January 2006 and July 2006 dealt extensively with the new library automation software, Challenger. The researcher can then return to these notes when preparing the final report and scan the January and July 2006 minutes where comments about the Challenger software are coded as "C-1," "C-2," etc.

Miles and Huberman (1994) recommend organizing the data into topics and files; reviewing the data for causes, consequences, and relationships; triangulating data with multiple sources and perspectives; developing design and evaluator checks; and recording stakeholder reactions to data and analyses. Russ-Eft and Preskill (2001) recommend reading and rereading the data; making notes; comparing and contrasting data with expectations, standards, or other frameworks; developing and assigning codes for each category; sorting the data by code; asking a colleague to code at least a portion of the data to determine inter-rater agreement or reliability; counting code frequencies; examining relationships between categories; and planning data displays (p. 324).

The case study researcher considers all of the data that have been collected. Each case analysis will include interview data, observational data, documentation data, statements, and impressions. Interpreting data analyses involves organizing all of the given information and making logical conclusions.

The case record organizes the raw data in a manageable form chronologically and thematically. The case study researcher is primarily concerned with analyzing the interview(s) and the observations. The researcher may write a case analysis for an interview with an individual and may also use this approach in writing about a program, group, or critical event as a single entity. The researcher will write a case study for each program unit using this approach. The researcher will use a cross-case analysis to group answers from different people, groups, or programs to common questions to analyze different perspectives on critical issues. The cross-case analysis often involves a synthesis of the data.

A standardized open-ended interview is the most useful method for organizing data for cross-case analysis. When variations in individuals or programs are the primary focus of the study, the researcher should write a case analysis for each individual or program before writing the cross-case analysis. For example, if one has interviewed 10 students who have completed library suggestion cards indicating their dissatisfaction with the library hours and various library services, the analysis may begin with a brief description of each student's individual experiences and frustrations before doing a cross-case analysis. However, if the focus is on satisfaction with the new library On-line Public Access Catalog (OPAC), the analysis may simply include a description of variations in answers to a survey interview about the new OPAC.

Patton (1990) recommends establishing a framework for organizing and analyzing observations. The six main frameworks are chronology, key events, various settings, people, processes, and issues. Chronological arrangements describe the case over time. Using a key events approach, the researcher presents the data by critical incidents or major events, usually in the order of importance rather than chronologically. Detailed descriptions of settings are important when the researcher is comparing settings and the effect of the environment on the case. If one individual is the focus of the case, then the researcher concentrates primarily on that person in reporting case data and his or her perceptions and reactions to other people and to the environment.

Organizational case studies typically focus on processes and the researcher will organize data to describe important processes. Impact studies and program implementation studies often focus on issues. Key issues and assessment data are the main focus of such studies.

Statistical or quantitative data may be reported or further analyzed for the purposes of the report. Appropriate matrices should be set up initially to record observations, interpretations, field comments, themes, and patterns.

It is important to allow the stakeholders the opportunity to review the data before they are placed in the final report. Site visit observations may be recorded and reviewed by different team members to gain a deeper, more objective perspective. Individuals involved in site visits should confirm data with the individuals that they have interviewed prior to preparing the final report. Ely et al. (1991) stress the importance of bracketing assumptions, feelings, and perceptions and striving to bracket them or put them aside in order to be open and receptive to the phenomenon, event, or program we are trying to understand.

Stake (1967) recommended preparing a Standards and Judgments Matrix. This simple matrix helps both the researcher and the stakeholders to recognize areas needing improvement. This instrument is intended to serve as a preliminary tool for identifying weaknesses and strengths. Some of the best examples of this type of matrices are found in Nelson and Fernekes (2002), *Standards and Assessments for Academic Libraries*. Another good source for standards matrices and forms is Brumley's, *The Academic Library Manager's Forms, Policies and Procedures Handbook*.

CODING THE DATA

Coding is assigning abbreviated designations to your data. You may use single words as codes, letters, numbers, phrases, symbols, or any combination of these items. Evaluation coding is appropriate for policy, critical, action, organizational, and evaluation studies (Saldana, 2009). The coding system should reflect the questions that initiated and structured the evaluation (Pitman & Maxwell, 1992). Coding occurs at two levels: identifying information about the data and interpretive constructs related to the analysis of the data (Merriam, 1998). Fink (2009) recommends keeping a code book for each evaluation. Sample code books are available on the Web. You can find some of these by searching under "surveys AND code book" or "+survey+codebook."

Case study researchers may choose to develop a system for coding their observations. For particularistic observations coding may involve making a list of the main issues and assigning numbers to each issue and then numbering each line on a page where the narrative is to be recorded. The researcher can go back and identify the line numbers from the narrative that correspond with the issue numbers. For example, Issue 1 is that a circulation attendant says "Get lost" to library patrons. The researcher observes the circulation attendant for a given period of time and records observations.

The researcher then goes back and notes the line numbers where the circulation attendant has said "Get lost" to a library patron and notes that on lines 5, 7, 11, 23, 29, 47, 53, and 81 of the report the circulation attendant has told someone to "get lost." Coding may involve using a tally sheet perhaps for reference questions. The main purpose of coding is for the researcher to develop a process or set of symbols that help efficiently and accurately record and report the narrative data. Coding becomes particularly important for comparative results with longitudinal case studies.

It is important to establish codes and categories early on in the study to remain consistent throughout the study. Merriam (1998) states that category construction is data analysis. The category names come from the researcher, participants, and literature. Categories should reflect the purpose of the research. Categories should be exhaustive, mutually exclusive, sensitizing, and conceptually congruent. Exhaustive categories help to place all data into a relevant category or subcategory. Mutually exclusive categories indicate that each piece of data can generally just be placed into one category.

Sensitizing category names enables the reader to have a clear sense of what data will be presented in each category because of the reader's familiarity with the category names. Conceptually congruent indicates that all categories share the same level of abstraction (Merriam, 1998). The main function of categories is to answer the who, what, when, and where questions of your research.

Russ-Eft and Preskill (2001) recommend guidelines for good category construction that include determining who will be involved in analyzing qualitative data, verifying data, making sure the categories reflect the chosen method of analysis, and attempting to create categories that are mutually exclusive. This also includes keeping careful notes about the decisions you make about why a certain kind of response goes in one category, developing a means for highlighting useful material you might wish to include in your final report, determining what you will do with vague comments, and developing a miscellaneous category for data that do not fit into any of the categories but that are relevant to the study's purpose (p. 324).

TRIANGULATION

Triangulation is an attempt on the part of the researcher to present a consistent framework for reporting the results. Triangulation involves coordinating current research in the field, institutional data, library documents and records, personal interviews and observations. Miles and Huberman (1994) recommend checking for obvious biases in the areas of representativeness, researcher effects, weighing the evidence using more robust measures, and feedback from informants. Throughout the case study the researcher must continually seek clarification and make sure that the event or individual is described accurately. The researcher needs to continually ask the question, How can this point be substantiated?

In some cases, evidence of an individual's behavior may be sufficiently documented by reporting additional incidents that confirm consistent reactions or behaviors. However, it is always best to provide quantitative data to confirm the researcher's suspicions whenever this is possible. When compiling the case study, develop some sort of symbol to use in the margin to indicate that the need to collaborate a behavior with evidence such as business records, absence records, or survey comments. The (delta) Δ symbol is often used by researchers to signify triangulation.

Fitzpatrick, Sanders, and Worthen (2004) differentiate between documents and records. **Documents** include personal or institutional records that have not been specifically prepared for research or investigation. Departmental minutes, organizational charts, policy and procedure manuals, and strategic plans document an institution's practices and procedures. They are generally prepared for departmental, interdepartmental, or institutional use. **Records** include official data summaries prepared for research or investigation by outside agencies. Accreditation reports, statistical data, and grant proposals would be examples of official records. Examining both documents and records is an important step in triangulating case findings within the bounds of a given context.

Triangulation is extremely important when we are discussing particularistic case studies because of the potential consequences involved if our findings and suppositions are not completely accurate. Triangulation is equally important when we are presenting a case study that is intended to be instrumental or instructive. When we are presenting an instrumental case study, we need to corroborate the implications of our case study with current literature, the campus or community milieu, experts in the field, institutional research, and library assessments. It is good to make notes of possible sources for triangulation as the researcher is writing. Sources may include people, studies, test scores, library assessment instruments, library consultants, and literature.

Lincoln and Guba (1985) recommend setting standards of confirmability and dependability in triangulating qualitative research results. They suggest that researchers should identify a list of sampling decisions made, both within and across cases, instrumentation and data collection operations, database summary, and software use. Hodson (1991) recommends establishing an account of constant comparative methods.

Lincoln and Guba (1985) discuss pattern theories in their research. The case study researcher identifies patterns or relationships among and between the data. Unlike causal theory, pattern theory does not always make logical sense. According to Neuman (1991), It does not require causal statements. Creswell (1994) discusses constantly comparing incidents until categories emerge. Yin (1989) recommends searching for patterns within the study to compare with conventional theory and the literature as a method for explanation building and performs time-series analysis to establish patterns over time. Young (1956) claims that the most meaningful quantitative studies are those linked with exhaustive case studies describing accurately the interrelationships of factors and processes.

Schwandt and Halpern (1988) recommend an auditing process for case studies addressing the grounding of the data, logical inferences, category structure, decision-making processes about methodological shifts, researcher bias, and inter-rater reliability. An extensive audit of this nature would be thorough and time consuming with a risk of dealing inappropriately with confidentiality issues in the process of verifying sources.

Complementarity

Triangulation deals with measuring the same construct or phenomenon. The researcher is looking at every angle of this one certain phenomenon and all of the documentation that point to conclusions about that phenomenon.

Complementarity may attempt to measure a different facet of the same construct, expecting to get different results but with the intent of learning about this different facet to provide a more complete picture. For example, researchers might examine the problems and issues that college students have using a new database. They might triangulate these findings with literature that is available on the use of this database from a nationwide sample. They could confirm findings using a survey and a focus group that has recently been conducted on campus. These additional data could be used to see if results are similar or different among college faculty. Asking the faculty a similar set of questions about the same database and examining the findings for similarities and differences would demonstrate this. The act of comparing the results from the two different groups would be complementarity. Complementarity typically utilizes a mixed-methods approach.

GOODNESS OF CASE STUDY RESEARCH

Van Dalen (1966) admonishes case study researchers to take great care when collecting evidence from records, interviews, and questionnaires to exercise every possible precaution to detect data that are the product of faulty perception, deliberate deception, a poor memory, unconscious biases, or the reporter's or subject's desire to present the right answer (p. 220). Van Dalen (1966) also emphasizes the tendency of the researcher to overemphasize unusual events to distort or dramatize the effect. In addition to triangulating case study data with conventional data sources, Marshall and Rossman (1995) recommend the tests of goodness for data collection. Such analysis and interpretation can be quite useful (pp. 146–148).

Case study research primarily involves observations, interviews, focus groups, and surveys. The following pages will focus specifically on collecting, analyzing, and interpreting these data.

Collecting, Analyzing, and Interpreting Observation Data

Observation data include *direct observations*, both *structured* and *unstructured*, and *site visits*. These help the researcher gain a more intense knowledge of program operations, participants' behaviors, reactions, and interactions.

Structured observations can involve inspecting or observing physical facilities as well as observing employees in a specific setting. Structured observations typically involve a preconceived notion or set of standards that are to be observed. For example, a librarian on an accreditation team may ask to see the new library addition or the new technology lab. This person might observe people interacting in these new spaces including furnishings, collections, and environmental factors such as climate control and lighting. The researcher may have a checklist of standards or criteria for conducting structured observations.

Unstructured observations may occur when an employee reacts to a comment at the water cooler or makes a passing comment in the hall. Unstructured observations are often informal opportunities that the researcher has to observe the stakeholders interacting with other participants. Unstructured observations include tone and intuition as well as direct comments. Sometimes these unstructured comments end up being tossed out as being irrelevant when the final report is composed; there are also times when it would behoove the researcher to follow up on some of these comments later with the appropriate stakeholders. Sometimes an impromptu comment may lead the researcher to request additional information or to confirm an earlier suspicion from a structured interview or observation.

The researcher's notes may be coded and categorized for later transcription. Some case study researchers do not like to be distracted by trying to take notes while they are observing and prefer to use a tape recorder, camcorder, or to have an assistant take notes. Researchers may sometimes take photographs or draw sketches to illustrate their narrative. These media may serve to enhance the presentation. It is important to check with the department of human subjects about campus policies regarding securing appropriate permissions and to carefully adhere to these guidelines.

Site visit observations are used by most accreditation and funding agencies to evaluate a program in its naturalistic setting. Stake (1970) noted that site visits are often criticized because visitors typically only see the best sides of programs. While it is certainly the intent of most institutions to show their best side during an evaluation, astute observers will request documentation and records that will help to form a balanced picture.

Fitzpatrick, Sanders, and Worthen (2004) recommend adequate preparation to enhance the usefulness of site visits. They recommend requesting specific information that will be needed, developing interview questions, developing on-site instruments, selecting on-site visitors, making pre-visit arrangements, conducting the on-site evaluation visit, and meeting with on-site administrators or staff to reemphasize the purpose, procedures, and expected products of the visit prior to the visit. Splitting the team up allows team members to cover more activities or interviewees. Regular debriefings are useful as is an exit interview with the site administrator(s) and, if appropriate, site staff. Adequate preparation and implementation aids in the writing and disseminating, and it will encourage actual use of the final report of the on-site evaluation (p. 379).

Collecting, Analyzing, and Interpreting Interview Data

Interviews often serve as an auxiliary method in conjunction with other methods in the evaluation process (Kvale & Brinkmann, 2009). Interviews help to clarify survey information and other data. Yin (2009) differentiates between in-depth interviews, focused interviews, and survey interviews. *In-depth interviews* involve asking key respondents about the facts of a matter as well as their opinions about key events and may actually involve several conversations with the interviewee to clarify facts and opinions. *Focused interviews* are conversational interviews that are designed to ask follow-up questions and to seek clarification about facts and events. These interviews typically involve limited access to a person or group and are generally onetime events. *Survey interviews* are conducted among key respondents to gain formalized data in an embedded case study.

Fitzpatrick, Sanders, and Worthen (2004) differentiate between exploratory, structured, and unstructured interviews. *Exploratory interviews* are preliminary interviews that the researcher schedules with the primary stakeholders in the beginning stages of the evaluation process to learn about their perspectives and concerns. *Structured interviews* are planned carefully with the interviewer asking specific questions that have been created ahead of time.

Structured interview questions are often follow-up questions from survey results or other data that the interviewee has previously provided. The interviewer is usually looking for specific information and will ask direct questions. *Unstructured interviews* are more general. The main goal of the interviewer in an unstructured interview is to make the interviewee feel comfortable in an effort to gain any relevant information. The interviewer may interview students informally and ask them general questions about the library or a new library program to obtain outcomes data in a narrative form.

Interview questions are of four types: essential, extra, background, and probing. Essential questions focus on the research questions or the central purpose of the study. Extra questions may be related to the essential questions and are usually asked as follow-up questions to the essential questions. Background questions are general, demographic, or background questions that serve to provide a context, and their main purpose is to put the interviewee at ease. Probing questions are designed to gather in-depth information about topics that an interviewee may raise or that the interviewer may seek answers to during an interview. Probing questions are generally not prepared prior to the interview (Berg, 1998).

Questions should be open-ended and use language that is familiar to the interviewee. They should be clear to the interviewee and neutral showing respect for the interviewee, and they are designed to generate answers related to the research questions and to the program objectives (Hatch, 2002).

The following general tips should be helpful in most interview situations: Jargon should be used sparingly; questions should be brief. Provide supplementary materials for interviewees and a specific frame of reference for your questions. Avoid suggesting answers, focus on the positive, and make the interviewee feel at ease.

Lincoln and Guba (1985) identify five outcomes of interviewing:

1. Here and now constructions—participant explanations of events, activities, feelings, motivations, concerns;
2. Reconstructions—explanations of past events and experiences;
3. Projections—explanations of anticipated experiences;
4. Triangulation—verification or extension of information from other sources; and
5. Member checking—verification or extension of information developed by the researcher.

Vaughn, Schumm, and Sinagub (1996) recommend allowing time before interviews to become acquainted with the participants. Provide participants with a brief overview of your expectations, start with an "icebreaker" building on the opening statements as guiding questions are addressed, keeping the conversation focused on the topic, encouraging participants to be specific and to use examples, monitoring and balancing participation, and giving a closing statement.

Hatch (2002) recommends focus groups for obtaining supplementary data in studies using observation and individual interviewing. These groups provide a means for capturing group opinions and attitudes toward a particular topic or program. Focus groups should rarely be used as a sole means for gathering data in support of a program or activity.

Collecting, Analyzing, and Interpreting Survey Data

When designing surveys, the evaluator should plan the questions, item types (Likert scale, multiple choice, or checklist), the number of items, and the analysis. Opinions and attitudes can generally be assessed with Likert scale items. Responses usually range from *strongly agree* to *strongly disagree*. Behaviors or preferences can be measured selecting multiple-choice items. Demographic data are usually determined with yes-no responses, open-ended questions, or short-answer items. Checklist items may be appropriate for determining levels of participation, specific services, or developing more thorough responses to previous questions.

Survey questionnaires should be thorough and yet not too wordy. Show respect for the respondent's time by constructing surveys that can will cover the data that are needed as succinctly as possible. The following are some tips for survey construction:

- Provide clear, concise instructions in an email or cover letter.
- Provide an explanation for the purpose of the survey and describe how and when the results will be distributed.
- Include information about who is sponsoring the survey.
- Distribute the survey to a small pilot group first to make sure that your instructions and questions are clear and sufficiently thorough. The pilot group should report on the length of time that the survey takes to complete.
- Review survey items to make sure that later responses are not biased by earlier questions, questions are grouped logically, there are no leading questions, the major issues are covered, questions are stated precisely, and definitions and terms are clear to the average respondent.

Fowler (2009) recommends a pre-survey evaluation. Respondents are asked to "think aloud" when they are responding to the pilot survey. They are then asked a set of follow-up questions related to their responses and any questions they may have had concerning the survey. Respondents may also be asked to state in their own words what the questions are asking and to explain why they chose one particular answer over another.

The analysis for a Likert or Likert-type survey generally involves providing descriptive data for each item and the total scores. Multiple-choice and checklist items just need to show percentages. Opinion items may be analyzed using t-tests and ANOVA.

Several books and websites provide an excellent basic coverage of Likert and many exercises that are a part of program evaluation. You may need to depend on the expertise of others on your team to help with statistics and other areas that may not be your area of expertise. It will be important for you to develop at least a rudimentary knowledge of statistical concepts to have meaningful conversations with other stakeholders about the statistics, statistical terms, and concepts that you choose to incorporate in your study. Jaisingh's (2000) *Statistics for the Utterly Confused* is a good resource. Another good resource is *Cliff's Quick Review: Statistics* by David Voelker (1993) and Peter Orton. The Statistics for Dummies website is another good resource: www.dummies.com/how-to/education-languages/math/statistics.html.

Interpreting survey responses involves either descriptive narrative or statistics measuring relationships among survey items. Modal statistics indicate the items that occur with the most frequency on a survey. Modal statistics can either be unimodal (having only one mode), bimodal (having two contrasting modes), or even trimodal (having three different modes). Unimodal responses give the researcher a clear understanding of the survey results. When there is more than one mode, the researcher needs additional information. Bimodal or even trimodal distributions may indicate a need for interviews or focus groups to gain a deeper understanding of responses that are not clear.

Cross-tabulation may be used to determine the relationship between two categories. Pivot tables in Excel are a good example of cross-tabulation. Cross-tabulation helps the researcher to look at specific categories and their relationships to various survey items. For example, a researcher might select one question and examine different variables such as gender, race, education level, income, or age. It is important to remember that a correlation between variables does not necessarily imply causation. One example that is frequently used to illustrate this fact is that there are typically more churches in high crime areas in most cities. However, we cannot say that churches cause crime. It is important to remember that statistics do not prove anything; they can only provide strong supporting evidence. The strength of causality between or among items can be inferred with more complicated statistical tests such as the ANOVA and regression analysis. When survey items indicate that one variable may be causing another, these results may be further interpreted using ANOVA tables. A paired t-test may be used to compare variables within each case. The objective would be to measure the statistical significance of the difference between two means when the variables are "paired" because the same respondents provided both responses (Alreck & Settle, 1985).

Correlation and regression analysis may be used to measure the degree, direction, and significance of relationships between two continuous, numeric variables when neither has been identified as being dependent or independent or no causality has been implied. Alreck and Settle (1985) recommend beginning with data description as well as organizing and interpreting the descriptions of individual variables before turning to measures of association. This may include averaging the results, recoding data and categories when necessary, treating continuous variables with only a few scale points as both continuous and categorical data for both description and measures of association, making inferences carefully, depending on cross-tabulation, and carefully checking causality and validity.

Collecting, Analyzing, and Interpreting Focus Group Data

Focus groups are a quick and relatively simple way for collecting group interview data during the planning and design stages of an evaluation. The main purposes of focus groups are to illicit openness, exploratory questions, and group interaction on an issue or topic. Focus groups are generally not appropriate to use as the only means for program evaluation.

Homogeneity generally works best to facilitate group interaction. Most experts recommend that focus group size should be between 6 and 12. The role of the leader or moderator is to facilitate group interaction and responses. The leader should never be someone who is in a supervisory role or holds an authoritative position over the focus group members. The moderator typically has an assistant to record responses on a large marker board. Focus group sessions are generally recorded and participants are compensated for their time. Focus group sessions usually last an hour or two. Both the moderator and the assistant observe body language and other nonverbal cues. Focus group results may be analyzed by themes for open-ended discussions or by responses to groups of questions posed by the moderator.

Collecting, Analyzing, and Interpreting Unobtrusive Data

Unobtrusive data help to corroborate other data. This type of data is usually defined as concrete examples or artifacts. Unobtrusive data include materials that may be collected without interrupting the routine or changing the environment in a rather informal manner. Attendance reports, informal conversations, previous surveys, memos, and personnel information would all be examples of unobtrusive data.

The researcher may wish to supplement some of the means of data that have been previously suggested with photographs, videotapes, audiotapes, examples of student work, and other unobtrusive data. It is important to remember to obtain appropriate permissions from any individuals involved in producing or serving as subjects for these sources of information.

CASE ANALYSIS METHODS

Case study researchers might wish to use some of the following types of analyses: cross-case analysis, multiple methods analysis, multiple case data, variable-oriented analysis, case-oriented analysis, and embedded analysis. Cross-case analysis of individual case studies has been the most common; however, aggregated groups may be studied as cases to yield validity to a case theory and assertions.

Cross-Case Analysis

Cross-case analysis shows patterns and similarities among individuals within a committee. For example, a researcher may choose to do a cross-case analysis of the management styles of Association of College and Research Library (ACRL) library directors. The researcher would identify common variables or traits among this group of library directors and would make appropriate assertions based on the similarities or differences among this group. His or her information might be helpful to trainers to prepare appropriate training materials for these librarians or to schools of library and information science in planning management courses.

Multiple Case Analysis

Denzin and Lincoln (1998) suggest that looking at multiple cases in multiple settings enhances generalizability, key processes, constructs, and that explanations can be tested in many different configurations. Using our information literacy example, we could interview several students at South Central and then interview students at 10 of South Central's benchmarking institutions, asking a uniform set of questions of each interviewee. The researcher should take note of the danger in overgeneralizing in cross-case analysis.

Gladwin (1989) and Miles and Huberman (1994) developed phenomenological composite cases using mixed strategies. Patton (1990) describes a synthesis study that focused on lessons learned about effective philanthropy from major grants based on a previous study by the McKnight Foundation. Synthesis studies typically involve case studies with a common focus.

Multiple Methods Research

Multiple methods research is essential in accurately interpreting data that are to be generalized to a larger population. Using the previous example, a researcher would want to use surveys, unobtrusive data, and perhaps focus groups to further interpret generalizations of data for university settings in general.

The case study researcher may either begin a cross-case analysis with the raw data or may complete individual case analysis for each case. The manner in which the researcher chooses to organize the data would depend on how much data are available and how the findings are to be presented.

Using multiple case data, the researcher will develop themes or categories to more efficiently organize the data. These themes may be derived from theoretical literature, an existing framework or schema, or the current data set.

When the researcher derives categories from the theoretical literature the intent is to provide support for a particular theory. The researcher may select themes or categories from technical literature or may use "in vivo codes." In vivo codes are words or themes that the researcher develops based on the interviewees' own words or institutional or organizational jargon. Two commonly used frameworks are *grounded theory* and *analytical induction*.

Glaser, the first proponent of grounded theory, recommended four steps in this research process: fit, relevance, workability, and modifiability. **Fit** occurs when the concepts or incidents are closely connected and can be compared using documentation that is available either unobtrusively or that becomes evident in the research process. **Relevance** indicates the level at which the research will apply to the outcomes of the study. **Workability** defines the application of the research in terms of everyday operations. Is the research practical or will it cause unnecessary interruptions in the work flow? **Modifiability** indicates the ability of the institution to use the findings to modify existing operations.

Grounded theory involves constantly comparing themes within the data from interviews, observations, narrative data, note-taking, and informal conversations. Unlike empirical data, grounded theory emerges as the case or evaluation unfolds in a naturalistic fashion.

Grounded theory involves using open coding and line-by-line analysis to dissect the data. The researcher is looking for themes within the data. Glaser and Strauss (1967) recommend applying the "constant comparative method" to compare theoretical literature with the data. Open coding breaks down the data into discrete parts, axial coding brings the data back together by making connections between the theme or category and subcategories (Strauss & Corbin, 1990). Axial coding involves identifying relationships among separate pieces of data. Axial coding may focus on conditions such as the context, actions, strategies, and consequences of actions.

Analytical induction involves using the same techniques as grounded theory. The researcher using this method formulates a theory about a situation or phenomenon and then examines the data for a fit between the theory and the actual data. The researcher continues comparing the data with the theory until a negative case is found. The purpose is to develop a theory that is sufficiently robust to handle all known cases. The researcher does not have to discard negative cases but must explain why they do not fit the theory.

The researcher derives categories from an existing framework or schema and is interested in placing the data in an organizational framework. Sometimes this approach is used in the initial phase of data analysis to coordinate the data with program objectives and to answer key evaluation questions.

The researcher deriving categories from the current data set tries to maintain objectivity by constantly comparing the preexisting data, current data, and theoretical literature. Russ-Eft and Preskill (2001) caution researchers using this approach to engage more than one analyst to determine a level of inter-rater agreement.

Variable-Oriented Analysis

The variable-oriented approach seeks to find common themes across cases. Researchers may use matrices containing adjectives that describe management styles, quantitative measures, organizational behavior, or leadership characteristics. Variable-oriented analysis is helpful in dissecting the usefulness of different variables in a study. For example, a researcher might include educational training as a variable in a case study of ACRL library directors. The researcher might note in the analysis that 100 percent of the library directors who graduated from a certain university had a certain management style and consistently exhibited a specific set of management traits.

Case-Oriented Analysis

The three common approaches to case-oriented analysis are replication strategy, grounded theory applied to multiple comparison groups, and multiple exemplars applied phenomenologically. All of these approaches may potentially yield valid results. The researcher must determine which approach is most appropriate for his or her case.

Yin (1989) advocates a replication strategy. The case study researcher establishes a conceptual framework for the first case study. Successive cases are examined for similarities within this same conceptual framework. This approach is also sometimes referred to as multiple case design (Powell & Connaway, 2004). Replication logic for multiple case studies differs from sampling logic and involves carefully selecting each case to predict similar results (literal replication) or predicting contrary results for predictable reasons (theoretical replication) (Yin, 1989). For example, Mr. White, a collection development librarian at Underdog University, might wish to do an analysis of his nursing collection to see if the library has a strong core nursing collection. Mr. White might check with faculty in the nursing department at his institution and, with bibliographic sources, conclude that the library has a strong core collection. Mr. White might then decide to do a comparative analysis of the nursing collection with a library with a similar size enrollment, in the same Carnegie class, and with a similar budget. Mr. White would expect these two collections to be similar. However, Mr. White's new Vice-President for Academic Affairs, Dr. Wysong, is highly ambitious.

Dr. Wysong wants to add a nurse practitioner program. Dr. Wysong attended Utopia University where she earned her undergraduate degree in nursing. She remembers the ideal nursing collection that was available at Utopia University and asks Mr. White to advise her of the budget that is needed to make Underdog University's nursing collection comparable to that of Utopia University.

Mr. White compares database records for both institutions, he interviews the collection development librarians at Utopia University, and he talks with the faculty at Underdog University who are planning the new nurse practitioner program and distributes questionnaires for them to identify program support materials for the new program. Mr. White is convinced from talking with other collection development librarians that these measures will be necessary to ascertain current needs, plan for the future, and to document collection building steps for the preliminary Nursing Board accreditation visit.

Some researchers argue that replicability is not possible because of real world changes and the uniqueness of individuals. Marshall (1995) concludes that researchers allow others to inspect their procedures, protocols, and decisions by keeping all collected data in well-organized, retrievable formats.

Glaser (1978) refines the replication construct by expanding case study research to multiple comparison groups. The original case and successive cases are examined for matching variables. A new library software company, Challenger, might wish to examine troubleshooting records for the new beta version of their Challenger software. Challenger is located on the West Coast and they have heard several complaints from customers on the East Coast that they are not receiving adequate support.

First, they decide to select the 10 institutions where they have received the highest number of complaints and determine that they will go to these institutions and review the case problems and interview the systems librarians at these institutions. They review their logs to determine the 10 institutions that they will visit and make careful notes of the complaints at each of these institutions. They interview the 10 systems librarians at these institutions, noting other problems such as climate control, user training, and systems support that may contribute to their software problems. The Challenger team compiles the data from these 10 libraries and attempts to synthesize the data looking for commonalities and differences.

The Challenger team then decides to interview a group of 10 universities on the West Coast of similar size with similar problems. They interview the 10 systems librarians at these institutions, noting other problems such as climate control, user training, and systems support that may contribute to their software problems. The Challenger team compiles the data from these 10 libraries and attempts to synthesize the data looking for commonalities and differences. They note that both groups of universities are reporting similar problems but that the East Coast libraries are reporting multiple case reports for the same problem because they are not receiving a timely response on problem reports logged in the mornings. They believe that the problem may be an issue because their offices are open from 10 a.m. until 6 p.m. Pacific Time. Based on these data they and are considering hiring an additional morning staff from 6 a.m. until 10 a.m. Pacific Time to accommodate customers on the East Coast.

Denzin (1989) uses multiple exemplars. He looks for essential elements that may be reconstructed to address a certain phenomenon. Denzin might, for example, interview a library director who had been convicted of embezzling library funds. It would not be necessary to interview every library director who had embezzled library funds, but a good representative sample as with any similar case. He might then do a number of other case studies involving library directors who have been convicted of embezzling library funds. He would then examine these studies for commonalities or multiple exemplars that might attempt to explain embezzling as a phenomenon. He would answer questions such as, "What personality traits do librarians have that embezzle money?" "What is the socioeconomic status of the typical librarian-embezzler?" "What are some of the reasons that the librarian-embezzler gives for committing this crime?" "What accounting and auditing practices were practiced at libraries where embezzling occurred?" "How long had the person been embezzling funds before she or he was caught?" "What is the typical sentence for a librarian who is convicted of embezzling funds?"

Patton (1990) advocated using multiple exemplars. Much can be learned from a few rich exemplars of the phenomenon in question.

Case-oriented analyses do not have to occur concurrently. A researcher may look at cases historically that have certain similarities. Case-oriented analyses are also known as object-oriented cases. The main point of case-oriented analyses is to review historic similarities among programs or cases.

Interpreting the Results

Draper (1988) suggests that explaining or interpreting the results may include providing requested information, justifying an action, giving reasons, supporting a claim, or making a causal statement. Using the information literacy case, the researcher will be using the data to justify an action, give reasons, and to support the claims of the librarians that information literacy helps students to become informed lifelong learners. The data will be used to answer several questions that have been suggested by the stakeholders.

Researchers draw their own conclusions on the basis of observations and other qualitative and quantitative data. Fitzpatrick, Sanders, and Worthen (2004) suggest the following questions that researchers should ask when using inferential statistics. What are the frequencies or, for continuous data, the shape of the distribution? Who are the "outliers"? What is the spread of the distribution? Are the respondents homogeneous or heterogeneous? Which options were selected more than anticipated? Which were selected less? All of this information would be discussed at length with the stakeholders. Their interpretations of the data would help to form the narrative that will be included in the final report.

When we are making assertions about a person's character, abilities, and attitudes in the process of writing a case study, we are obligated to prove our case much like attorneys who produce evidence to prove the guilt or innocence of their clients in the courtroom. As has been stated earlier in this chapter, it is important to remember that statistics do not prove anything; they can only provide strong supporting evidence. The researcher must provide enough supporting evidence to make a strong case for the opinion that is being presented.

Ragin (1987) concludes that researchers are free to make assertions only after they have tested a theory; all of the relevant data have been examined, any irrelevant data have been removed; and there has been a steady and explicit "dialogue" between ideas and evidence. Grounded theory and other theories that we have discussed help the researcher to maintain a constant and explicit dialogue between ideas and evidence.

Denzin and Lincoln (1998) address the issue of causality in case study research. They argue that qualitative studies are especially well suited to establishing causal relationships because they directly examine the case and underlying events and show how specific outcomes were achieved, ruling out rival hypotheses.

Case studies are sometimes longitudinal, providing the researcher with a stable set of data over time. For example, South Central might compare grade point averages of students who took the information literacy course over a four-year period.

Mixed strategies that combine analysis techniques have been used by some researchers to achieve a composite case study. Gladwin (1989) and Miles and Huberman (1994) developed phenomenological composite cases using mixed strategies. Patton (1990) describes a synthesis study that focused on lessons learned about effective philanthropy from major grants based on a previous study by the McKnight Foundation. Synthesis studies typically involve case studies with a common focus.

Creswell (1998) discusses holistic analysis as an effort on the part of the researcher to incorporate the views of the organization as well as his or her own views. In recording the views of the organization, the researcher may include an overview of the history, politics, economy, and environment that have bounded the case.

Russ-Eft and Preskill (2001) state that in evaluating learning, performance, and changing initiatives, the goal would be to construct a holistic understanding or gestalt of the organization members' context. It would be important to understand the meanings associated with learning, performance, or change as a result of some intervention or initiative for a particular individual or organization.

Case studies using multiple methods and sources of data would be most useful for determining the success of an intervention or change within an organizational context. Gaining a full or holistic picture involves studying the context, understanding the situation, seeking multiple sources of evidence, and using assessment questions that focus on the "how" and "why" of something. Generalizing findings is not usually the goal of a holistic case study analysis.

Embedded Analysis

Embedded analysis focuses on a specific aspect of the case (Yin, 1989). Within case analysis focuses on themes within the case and a cross-case analysis focuses on common themes but may make assertions or causative interpretations (Creswell, 1998). Patton (1990) discusses the importance of developing a sensitivity for observing alternative explanations and patterns that would invalidate initial insights. This holism is sometimes called embedded analysis. Discussing the alternative explanations and patterns as part of the whole case will provide the stakeholders with a richer, thicker description and a more relevant one than could otherwise be presented.

Glaser (1978) and other grounded theorists have contended that slices of data from many different sources are much more compelling than data from one source. Triangulating these multiple data sources to validate findings is a responsible practice for the case study researcher.

A library director may review a case study that has been written about a library employee (Mary). The case study was prepared as documentation for Mary's termination. The library director wants to make certain that she has covered all of her bases and has kept a complete paper trail. The case study might indicate that Mary has failed to complete assigned tasks, has not attended departmental meetings, has stolen funds from petty cash, and has claimed that she cannot lift books because of her back condition.

The director decides to check the following sources to collaborate the case study narrative. She calls Mary's supervisor and asks how many days Mary has been absent in the last three months. Mary's supervisor reports that Mary has been absent 33 days in the last three months. The director is astounded and asks if Mary has an illness. Mary's supervisor responds that she is not aware of any particular illness and also mentions that she has asked her to bring documentation to confirm her back problem. Mary has never provided any documentation from her doctor but continues to insist that she cannot lift books. Mary's supervisor also volunteered to provide the director with a specific list of tasks that she had assigned Mary a month ago and documentation that none of these tasks had been completed.

The director also calls the library office administrator who confirms that on the days that Mary worked at the circulation desk, the petty cash funds did not balance. The library director also reviews copies of the minutes from Mary's department. The minutes confirm that Mary had not attended meetings for her department.

Corroborating case study observations with multivariate research or mixed methodologies is a major key to establishing credibility as a case study researcher. While it is important to provide strong supporting evidence for projects that involve large capital funding expenditures and human resources, it is even more critical to make a good case for particularistic case studies.

Yin (2009) recommends maintaining a chain of evidence to increase the reliability of the case study. The individual elements of this chain of evidence have been discussed in earlier chapters. The chain of evidence begins with the case study questions, the case study protocol links questions to protocol topics, citations should be provided to specific evidentiary sources in the case study database, and the case study database then provides the material for the case study report. The stakeholders or the researchers can then backtrack and review any of the individual components of this chain to gain a fuller picture of the whole case. This chain of evidence helps to ensure quality control throughout the evaluation of the program or case.

CASE APPLICATION

The synergy was back; the whole committee gathered to design the evaluation. The librarians had agreed to share lesson plans that were based on the ACRL Information Literacy Competency Standards. The librarians and several faculty members had agreed to share student papers, projects, and scores from pre- and posttests. They would share minutes from the ad hoc information literacy committee and from the curriculum committee meetings where the ACRL standards were discussed during the formative stages.

A classroom observation instrument for some of the committee members to observe the information literacy class was developed. The instrument was somewhat open-ended. The main purpose was to determine the methods for instruction and to observe how students respond.

We developed some interview questions based on the program evaluation questions. We might add others that will be suggested by the focus group. We set up a tentative interview schedule to interview administrators, faculty, and students. We discussed that we would use purposeful sampling to make sure that we included individuals from all of these committees that were familiar with the information literacy curriculum. We talked about the focus group. Jason Norman is going to invite a friend from a nearby university with a similar program to facilitate the focus group.

We developed a survey for students with Likert-scale items to determine attitudes toward the information literacy program. The librarians will select a small committee to pilot-test the survey. We are still working on a survey for administrators and faculty. We have determined a list of university documents that we will review such as the strategic plan.

Dr. Sanders has volunteered to provide a list of benchmarking institutions and the librarians are aware of three of these institutions that have recently implemented similar information literacy programs. The librarians are going to coordinate a study with these

(continued)

other three libraries that will include the survey, interviews, and a focus group. All three institutions will use the same questions that will be used at South Central.

We made sure that we had developed appropriate categories, analysis methods, and scales for all of our data. I especially emphasized making sure that our observation and interview questions matched the program evaluation questions. I did not want there to be any glitches with the analysis.

We agree that all of the data and analyses will be stored in my office in a locked filing cabinet. I reiterated to the committee the importance of maintaining confidentiality. Someone mentioned reviewing absenteeism for the information literacy course and to compare records with other elective courses.

I am wondering if Dr. Porter will back down and allow Dr. Anderson to incorporate the findings from her study. I need to talk with her again.

I really missed Dr. Sanders at our meeting today. He could have contributed a lot to our discussion on program design. I also missed the other library staff. Dr. Walters shows little enthusiasm even though I have tried to draw her in. She and Dr. Porter are clearly present only physically. They have been discussing a previous strategic planning meeting among themselves and seem to be tuning out the rest of the committee. Dr. Porter had quickly explained that the committee would be smaller from now on because Drs. Sanders and Anderson were busy with "more important tasks and the librarians needed to be in the library because they were understaffed."

Everyone else seemed excited about the design phase. We have talked about the design previously and now it is a matter of deciding how we will analyze the content of the various in-house documents that we have available and the content of the interviews, observations, focus group comments, and other unobtrusive data. Some of the evaluation questions simply ask for descriptive information. These are designed to inform the stakeholders about the program and information literacy competency standards. The other questions were clearly linked to outcomes.

I am convinced more than ever that a case study is needed to stimulate dialogue between the diverse groups on this campus and to bring about unified strategic planning. Just as I was talking with the committee about coordinating the focus group findings with the interviews and using the focus group exercise as an opportunity to form meaningful interview questions, a tall, distinguished gentleman entered the room and introduced himself as Dr. Archer, the university president.

Dr. Archer politely asked if he could join the committee. Drs. Porter and Walters were obviously taken aback by Dr. Archer's unannounced appearance. They quickly put a graph away that they had been discussing from a previous meeting. Dr. Archer explained to the committee that he had seen Jason Norman at lunch and he had talked to him about the information literacy program. "This guy is sharp. We are really fortunate to have him. This information literacy program is exactly what we have needed on this campus for a long time. I hope you don't mind me intruding but I just wanted to learn more about the program and this evaluation process."

I cordially welcomed Dr. Archer and briefly explained our planning efforts to this point. I gave him copies of the matrices that we had developed and explained that we were in the process of fine-tuning our data analysis and interpretation procedures. "Where is Dr. Sanders?" Dr. Archer questioned. "He should be in on this committee."

Dr. Porter was clearly embarrassed. "Dr. Sanders has too many other commitments," she volunteered. Dr. Archer took out his cell phone. "I'm going to call him. I know that he would make time for this. I'll see about giving him an extra stipend if we need to do so."

While Dr. Archer was waiting for Dr. Sanders to answer, he quickly scanned to room. "It looks like *Jason* and some of those librarians that have been teaching this course should be involved in this planning thing too. What do you think?" He was directing his question toward me. Again, I could see that Dr. Porter was uncomfortable.

I tried to answer in a guarded manner. "I will defer to Dr. Porter and to the rest of the committee for deciding who should serve on the committee." One committee member spoke up, "They were originally on the committee and if they have time to serve, we sure need them." Dr. Archer's wheels were still clicking.

"Dr. Porter, didn't Dr. Anderson present some report and I think she published it in a peer-reviewed journal too about this program and retention rates?" Dr. Porter acknowledged that Dr. Anderson had in fact presented her paper at a national conference and had published it in *The Journal of Learning Disabilities*.

Dr. Archer asked Dr. Porter why Dr. Anderson had not been asked to serve on this committee. Dr. Porter offered her excuse that executive level people were too busy with other university matters to serve on this committee. One of the professors spoke up and mentioned that she had been on the committee initially too. Dr. Archer appeared to be puzzled by this news but proceeded to call Dr. Anderson also.

Drs. Porter and Walters were obviously annoyed by this turn of events but I was almost literally jumping up and down for joy. I felt like we would have all of the main stakeholders back at the table. I just hoped that we could somehow see some support from Drs. Porter and Walters. I thought that it would be best to hold off on any further planning until we could bring these other individuals back to the table. I suggested that we go ahead and call it a day and reconvene with the whole committee the following day at the same time to continue with our planning.

Describe how the committee should design the evaluation. Do you have any ideas for convincing Drs. Porter and Walters about the importance of the information literacy program and helping them to get beyond their political interests?

APPLICATION QUESTIONS AND EXERCISES

1. When would an interview be an appropriate method for gathering information in the South Central study?
2. Do you think that face-to-face, telephone, or computer-generated interviews would be most appropriate for each of the individuals or instances that you have listed?
3. Discuss the advantages and disadvantages associated with collecting observation data for the South Central study.
4. Design a brief interview for fellow classmates or coworkers about a class or their job. Interview at least three individuals.
5. What are the differences in their responses? What are the similarities?
6. Did you notice any changes in your interview style with any of these individuals? Why?
7. Was an interview the best way to answer these questions or would a survey or focus committee have been more appropriate?

8. What documents or records might be useful where you work for an evaluation?
9. What documents or records might you request for the South Central study?
10. Develop a survey to measure attitudes toward work in your department or toward your class.
11. Pilot test your survey on a small group and discuss the responses and interpretations.
12. How will you revise your questions?
13. Will you continue to use the survey or another method for gathering this information? If not, what method(s) will you use?

MAJOR CHAPTER THEMES

The three common approaches to case-oriented analysis are replication strategy, grounded theory applied to multiple comparison groups, and multiple exemplars applied phenomenologically. All of these approaches may potentially yield valid results. The researcher must determine which approach is most appropriate for his or her case. Interpreting may include providing requested information, justifying an action, giving reasons, supporting a claim, or making a causal statement.

The selection of methods, the analysis, and the interpretation are all dependent on the nature of the evaluation questions and the context of the program being evaluated. Interviews, observations, documents and records, test scores, questionnaires, and focus groups all provide valuable pieces of data to the program evaluation puzzle.

Qualitative data are analyzed using patterns and themes. Categories may be formed and revised as information is collected and emerges. Quantitative data are analyzed using descriptive and inferential statistics. Data should be interpreted as well as analyzed.

CHAPTER EVALUATION STANDARDS

Review the Joint Committee on Standards for Educational Evaluation (1994) in Appendix A. Describe the standards that are relevant to this chapter.

REFERENCES

Alreck, P., & Settle, R. *The Survey Research Handbook.* Homewood, IL: Irwin, 1985.

Berg, B. *Qualitative Research Methods for Social Sciences.* Boston: Allyn & Bacon, 1998.

Creswell, J. *Qualitative Inquiry and Research Design: Choosing Among Five Traditions.* Thousand Oaks, CA: Sage, 1998.

Creswell, J. *Research Design: Qualitative and Quantitative Approaches.* Thousand Oaks, CA: Sage, 1994.

Denzin, N. *Interpretive Biography. Qualitative Research Methods,* 17. Thousand Oaks: Sage, 1989.

Denzin, N., & Lincoln, Y. *Collecting and Interpreting Qualitative Materials.* Thousand Oaks: Sage, 1998.

Draper, S. What's Going on in Everyday Explanation? In C. Antaki (Ed.), *Analyzing Everyday Explanations: A Casebook of Methods.* Newbury Park, CA: *Sage,* 1988.

Ely, M., Anzul, M., Friedman, T., Garner, D., & Steinmetz, A. *Doing Qualitative Research: Circles within Circles.* London: Falmer, 1991.

Fink, A. *How to Conduct Surveys: A Step-by-Step Guide,* 4th ed. Thousand Oaks, CA: Sage, 2009.

Fitzpatrick, J., Sanders, J., & Worthen, B. *Program Evaluation Alternative Approaches and Practical Guidelines,* 3rd ed. Boston: Allyn & Bacon, 2004.

Fowler, F. *Survey Research Methods*, 4th ed. Thousand Oaks, CA: Sage, 2009.

Gladwin, C. *Ethnographic Decision Tree Modeling*. Thousand Oaks, CA: Sage, 1989.

Glaser, B. *Theoretical Sensitivity*. Mill Valley, CA: Sociology Press, 1978.

Glaser, B., & Strauss, A. *The Discovery of Grounded Theory*, Chicago: Adeline, 1967.

Hatch, J. *Doing Qualitative Research in Educational Settings*. Albany, NY: SUNY Press, 2002.

Hodson, R. The Active Worker. *Journal of Contemporary Ethnography*, Vol. 20, (1) (1991): 47–78.

Jaisingh, L. Statistics for the Utterly Confused. McGraw-Hill: New York, 2000.

Joint Committee on Standards for Educational Evaluation. *The Program Evaluation Standards*, 2nd ed. Thousand Oaks, CA: Sage, 1994.

Kvale, S., & Brinkmann, S. *Interviews: Learning the Craft of Qualitative Research Interviewing*. 2nd ed. Thousand Oaks, CA: Sage, 2009.

Lincoln, Y. S., & Guba, E. *Naturalistic Inquiry*. Beverly Hills, CA: Sage, 1985.

Marshall, C., & Rossman, G. *Designing Qualitative Research*, 2nd ed. Thousand Oaks, CA: Sage, 1995.

Merriam, S. *Qualitative Research and Case Study Applications in Education*. San Francisco: Jossey-Bass, 1998.

Miles, M., & Huberman, A. *Qualitative Data Analysis*, 2nd ed. Thousand Oaks, CA: Sage, 1994.

Nelson, W., & Fernekes, R. *Standards and Assessment for Academic Libraries: A Workbook*. Chicago: ALA, 2002.

Neuman, W. *Social Research Methods: Qualitative and Quantitative Approaches*. Boston: Allyn & Bacon, 1991.

Patton, M. The Challenge of Being Professional. *Evaluation Practice, 9* (1990): 5–24.

Pitman, M., & Maxwell, J. Qualitative Approaches to Evaluation: Models and Methods. In M. D. LeCompte, W. L. Millroy, & J. Preissle (eds.), *The Handbook and Qualitative Research in Education*, 729–770. San Diego: Academic Research Press, 1992.

Powell, R., & Connaway, L. *Basic Research Methods for Librarians*, 4th ed. Library and Information Science Text Series. Westport, CT: Libraries Unlimited, 2004.

Ragin, C. *The Comparative Method. Moving Beyond Qualitative and Quantitative Strategies*. Berkeley: University of California Press, 1987.

Russ-Eft, D., & Preskill, H. *Evaluation in Organizations*. Cambridge, MA: Perseus, 2001.

Saldana, J. *The Coding Manual for Qualitative Researchers*. Thousand Oaks, CA: Sage, 2009.

Schwandt, T., & Halpern, E. *Linking Auditing and Metaevaluation: Enhancing Quality in Applied Research*. Beverly Hills, CA: Sage, 1988.

Stake, R. *The Art of Case Study Research*. Thousand Oaks, CA: Sage, 1995.

Stake, R. The Countenance of Educational Evaluation. *Teacher's College Record, 68* (1967): 523–540.

Stake, R. Objectives, Priorities, and Other Judgment Data. *Review of Educational Research, 40* (1970):181–212.

Strauss, A., & Corbin, J. *Basics of Qualitative Research: Grounded Theory Procedures and Techniques*. Thousand Oaks, CA: Sage, 1990.

Van Dalen, D. *Understanding Educational Research*. New York: McGraw-Hill, 1966.

Vaughn, S., Schumm, J., & Sinagub, J. Focus Group Interviews in Education and Psychology. Newbury Park, CA: Sage, 1996.

Voelker, D., & Orton, P. *Cliff's Quick review (Statistics)*. Cliff's Notes: Lincoln, NE, 1993.

Yin, R. *Case Study Research: Design and Methods*. Thousand Oaks, CA: Sage, 1989.

Yin, R. K. *Case Study Research: Design and Methods, 4th ed*. Thousand Oaks, CA: Sage, 2009.

Young, P. *Scientific Social Surveys and Research*. Englewood Cliffs, NJ: Prentice-Hall, 1956.

10

Reporting the Case Study

FOCUS QUESTIONS

What are some of the main purposes of the evaluation report?

Describe the importance of the executive summary and the material that should be included in the executive summary.

How would you organize the report for the stakeholders in the South Central study?

As discussed in earlier chapters, evaluation reports can serve numerous purposes. Evaluation reports may serve as:

- measures of accountability,
- decision-making tools,
- a means to investigate a topic of interest,
- a tool for convincing stakeholders to take action,
- planning or policy data,
- an impetus for change in attitudes or behaviors, or
- a means for introducing new ideas.

WRITING THE FINAL EVALUATION REPORT

Writing the final evaluation report should be a matter of pulling together the data sources into a meaningful whole. If the researcher has carefully attended to details during each stage of the data collection and analysis stages, writing the findings is a matter of putting the stories in their final form and providing readers with enough information to make sense of the narrative being presented (Hatch, 2002).

ORGANIZATION OF THE FINAL EVALUATION REPORT

Your report should be organized in the following way. The design chapter discussed the importance of involving the client, stakeholders, and participants in the evaluation design. One of the reasons for their involvement is to ensure that they will help to form an evaluation structure that will produce results that are meaningful to them in the end. The reporting structure should be a mirror image of the design. The report should reflect the information that the client, stakeholders, and participants had requested initially in their questions and other design mechanisms.

KEY COMPONENTS OF THE FINAL EVALUATION REPORT

The final evaluation report includes several essential components. The researcher will provide an executive summary, brief introduction to the report, the focus of the evaluation, a brief overview of evaluation plan and procedures, a presentation of evaluation results, conclusions and recommendations, minority reports or rejoinders (if any), and the appendices (Fitzpatrick, Sanders, & Worthen, 2004).

Executive Summary

The executive summary is a brief summary of critical information that is usually included as the first page of the report. Rubin and Rubin (2005) suggests thinking about the executive summary as the condensed version that you might give an individual who does not have time to read the entire report and just wants a few brief sentences or paragraphs that describe your research.

The executive summary is often printed on different color paper and sometimes a heavier weight paper than the rest of the report. The executive summary is generally less than five pages and, in most cases, only two pages.

The executive summary briefly outlines the study's purpose, the methods that were used, and a summary of the data that were collected. Major findings and recommendations are often bulleted or numbered. Sometimes the executive summary will be displayed on a website, posters, and brochures or in other formats for more general audiences who just need to have a synopsis of the report. In some cases, the executive summary may be reduced even further to an executive abstract.

Report Introduction

The introduction to the report briefly outlines the basic purpose(s) of the evaluations. This includes the audience, the rationale, and disclaimers or comments about the limitations of the report, and where the case study is conducted.

Focus of the Evaluation

The focus of the evaluation section will include the rationale, goals and objectives, strategies and procedures, and the evaluation design. The evaluation questions and other structures that helped to frame the evaluation will be included in this section. It is good to include the procedures for collecting, analyzing, and reporting the evaluation data.

Evaluation Plan Overview

The overview section will contain the evaluation plan describing the data collection instruments, methods, and the data analysis techniques. The overview section should contain a summary of the instruments and methods used. The actual instruments may be included in the appendix or be available through Web links or other means.

Presentation of Results

The results section includes the results, conclusions, and recommendations based on the evaluation data that were collected. Data may be presented in tables, graphs, displays, and in other forms in the written report or on a website. The results section is the culmination of all of the data that have been collected, interpreted, and analyzed with the involvement of representative groups from the entire organization. Since everyone has participated in the complete project, the final results should be a culminating event that does not involve any unpleasant surprises for anyone.

Conclusions and Recommendations

The evaluator should list the standards that were used to develop conclusions and recommendations. Again, the client and stakeholders should have all agreed on these standards in the initial design stages of the evaluation. Focus attention on both positive and negative statements with the strengths being listed first. Some evaluators use a SWOT format for this section. If this format is used, the report may serve a dual role in strategic planning efforts.

Minority Reports or Rejoinders

Minority reports or rejoinders are not always necessary. However, if there should be a strong dissenting opinion among one group, it is good to represent their view by preparing a brief report outlining their concerns and dissenting opinions with regard to the final report.

Appendices

Information such as the actual survey instruments should be placed in the appendices for the study. If the administration of the university has written a detailed letter requesting the study, it could be placed in the appendix to support the implementation of any results.

The evaluator will want to accommodate all of the different audiences in preparing the report. The level of detail, technical writing style, and the appearance of the report should all reflect the particular audience for which the report is being prepared. If there is an oral presentation the audience should be involved in the presentation and should have opportunities to ask questions and to discuss the results.

COMPLETION AND DISTRIBUTION OF THE FINAL REPORT

The same individuals who were involved in the initial design should have the opportunity to review interim and draft reports and to request corrections and additions. The evaluator should always allow adequate time for individuals to read and to respond with feedback either orally or in written form. Evaluators should make sure to take the time to incorporate the feedback that is provided and to treat all individuals with respect during this process.

The information in the report may be presented in different formats depending on the preferences of the client, stakeholders, and participants and the abilities of the evaluator. Some common formats include written reports, multimedia presentations, poster board displays, graphic displays, and Web-based presentations. Different audiences may request different types of presentations and may assist in the technical development of the reports. Different audiences may receive more extensive information or a condensed version based on their level of interest and involvement. Shorter, targeted versions with basic, summary information may be prepared for students and general audiences. Longer, more intensive versions can be made available for executive stakeholders.

CONCLUSIONS

The case study researcher reviews the matrices, supporting data, and field notes and states the conclusions from these findings. The researcher carefully validates his or her research findings using all available data. The researcher will reiterate initial research questions in the concluding remarks and will address any new questions that have arisen from the current case study.

CASE APPLICATION

> The committee submitted all of its individual reports and data to me for compiling the final report. I have promised the committee that I will distribute the final draft of the report to them the last week in March. I will prepare a PowerPoint presentation and a written report with an executive summary. I will give them the written report and the executive summary a few days before we meet.
>
> After I have the PowerPoint presentation ready, we will have a meeting so that they can inform me of any changes or additions that need to be made before I compile the final report. I will then place the executive summary on the library website and the librarians will prepare some brochures. Are there any other key elements that my final report should include?
>
> Incidentally, I just learned that Dr. Walters has resigned and will be going back to the library where she worked before coming to South Central University.

APPLICATION QUESTIONS AND EXERCISES

1. Discuss the advantages and disadvantages of different types of report presentations (i.e., written report, brochures, webpage).
2. What are some things that you would recommend for preparing an effective report?

MAJOR CHAPTER THEMES

Evaluation reports serve numerous purposes. The evaluator should clearly identify the audience(s) when preparing the report. All of the appropriate individuals should be involved throughout the planning and evaluation process to ensure a smooth reporting session.

Evaluation reports may be presented via many different formats for different audiences. Final reports should include certain key elements.

CHAPTER EVALUATION STANDARDS

Review the Joint Committee on Standards for Educational Evaluation (1994) in Appendix A. Describe the standards that are relevant to this chapter.

REFERENCES

Fitzpatrick, J., Sanders, J., & Worthen, B. *Program Evaluation Alternative Approaches and Practical Guidelines*, 3rd ed. Boston: Allyn & Bacon, 2004.

Hatch, J. *Doing Qualitative Research in Education Settings*. State University of New York Pr.: New York, 2002.

Rubin, H., & Rubin, I. *Qualitative Interviewing: The Art of Hearing Data*, 2nd ed. Thousand Oaks, CA: Sage, 2005.

11

Data Analysis Software and Matrices

A number of qualitative software programs are available. Just as there are no specific constructs or formulas for conducting qualitative research, there are no specific programs that best analyze qualitative research. Each program has built in assumptions based on individual software developer's preferences and theories. Weitzman and Miles (1995) note some of the advantages of using computer data analysis software. These advantages include coding data by attaching keywords, linking data, storing and organizing data, searching and retrieving similar data, counting data using code frequencies or sequences, and displaying data graphically.

The researcher will still need to establish the codes that are to be used and enter relevant data for analysis. Miles and Huberman (1994) have developed a useful table of program characteristics for qualitative software (p. 316).

ENTERING QUALITATIVE DATA

Qualitative data are usually entered and saved in ASCII format. Questionnaires and other prestructured data may be entered into a spreadsheet program, such as Excel. Each line can represent one respondent, and each column the answer to one question.

SPEECH RECOGNITION SOFTWARE

Speech recognition programs are helpful when transcribing long narratives. Microsoft has a built in speech recognition tool that works much like Naturally Speaking and Via Voice. This option may be accessed by clicking on the control panel, then choosing the control panel icon "Speech," and then selecting "Speech Properties." A tutorial is offered to train the researcher voice to Microsoft and to train the researcher to use the product. The other three main speech recognition software companies are Naturally Speaking, published by Dragon Dictate, Voice Direct, and Via Voice, from IBM.

The researcher trains the computer to understand the researcher voice and speak into a microphone. The highlighted words appear on the screen. This software may be used for group discussions on the researcher laptop. It will only record the voice that it has been trained for so the user must still type other comments that are to be included in the transcript.

SOFTWARE FOR ANALYZING QUALITATIVE DATA

Qualitative software does not analyze text as SPSS or Minitab do for quantitative data. Unlike quantitative packages that are all quite similar, qualitative software requires different skill levels and is designed to accomplish entirely different purposes. It is important to select a program that will fit your needs so that you do not constantly have to learn new software. Most qualitative research data has a steep learning curve.

WORD PROCESSING SOFTWARE

Most word-processing programs offer options for outlining, word counting, pattern-searching, and sorting. Nisus and BBEdit are designed for Macintosh users. Nisus features such as read/write documents in Unicode, RTF, RTFD, plain text format, and Microsoft Word (.doc); a customizable interface; AppleScript and Perl macros; non-contiguous selection; keyboard shortcuts; an exclusive Document Manager; powerful, three-level Find and Replace including Regular Expressions (GREP); multiple editable clipboards; and document window zoom. These features make Nisus Writer Express a good choice for ethnographic researchers.

BBEdit is most useful for Web authors and software developers. This award-winning product has editing, searching, and text manipulation features. An intelligent interface provides easy access to BBEdit's best-of-class features including group pattern matching, search and replace across multiple files, function navigation and syntax coloring for source code languages, FTP and SFTP open and save, AppleScript, Perl and Mac OS X UNIX scripting support, support and a complete set of HTML tools.

SOFTWARE FOR LINKING CONCEPTS

Most researchers complete a series of interviews, transcribe them, and enter the transcripts into a software program. This process enables the researcher to label statements, categorize them, and to draw appropriate conclusions.

NVivo software can examine textual information such as in-depth interviews and focus group transcripts, documents, and field or case notes. NVivo can be used for a wide range of research including network and organizational analysis, action or evidence-based research, discourse analysis, grounded theory, conversation analysis, ethnography, literature reviews, phenomenology, and mixed methods research. It specializes in manipulating words and text. NVivo has a discussion list. It is important to find out what sort of user networking capabilities are available with any software.

Two other programs similar to NVivo are ATLAS.ti and The Ethnograph. ATLAS.ti allows links between related data. ATLAS.ti includes Object Managers, the Network Editor, the Object Explorer, the Code Forest, and the Code Tree. These tools help the researcher to browse and navigate through data structures and concepts. Other tools, such as the Hermeneutic Unit (HU) Editor, the Text Editors, and the Memo tool help with reading, annotating, and writing during the researcher analytical process. Text Search Tool, the Auto Coding Tool (Auto Coder), the Object Crawler, and the Query

Tool are available for searching. The SPSS Export function and the Word Cruncher enable the researcher to bridge the qualitative-quantitative gap. Teamwork and collaborative projects are provided with the User Administration tool, the HU Merger, the Redundant Coding Analyzer, and the HTML and XML generators.

The Ethnograph is designed to import text-based qualitative data straight into the program. The Ethnograph helps the researcher search and note segments of interest within the researcher data, mark them with code words and run analyses that can be retrieved for inclusion in reports or further analysis.

CDC EZ-Text is a software program developed to assist researchers in creating, managing, and analyzing semi-structured qualitative databases. Researchers can design a series of data entry templates tailored to their questionnaire. These questionnaires are usually administered during face-to-face interviews with a sample of respondents. A response to a question may be entered into EZ-Text either as a verbatim transcript from a tape recording or a summary generated from the interviewer's notes. Data from respondents can be typed directly into the templates or copied from word-processor documents. Following data entry, investigators can interactively create online codebooks, apply codes to specific response passages, develop case studies, conduct database searches to identify text passages that meet user-specified conditions, and export data in a different format for further analysis with other qualitative or statistical analysis software programs. Project managers can merge data files generated by different interviewers for combined cross-site analyses. The ability to export and import the codebook helps to coordinate the efforts of multiple coders simultaneously working with copies of the same database file. Additional EZ-Text features include importing text files and Reliability Agent, which calculates statistics and generates reports for the degree of agreement between two coders, Data Export, Database Merge, and Database Subset Agents.

HyperRESEARCH is an easy-to-use qualitative data analysis software package enabling the researcher to code and retrieve, build theories, and conduct analyses of the researcher data. HyperRESEARCH allows the researcher to work with text, graphics, audio, and video sources. HyperRESEARCH provides coding of any type of source, including text, audio, video, and image files. HyperRESEARCH has a unique case-based approach presenting the researcher data the way the researcher collected it. It includes analysis tools and for integration of cases from multiple study files.

HyperTRANSCRIBE lets the researcher transcribe nearly any audio or video file, with keyboard shortcuts that keep the researcher's fingers close to the "home row" the researcher can transcribe on any Windows or Mac OS computer. Customizable shortcuts let the researcher enter blocks of text in a single keystroke. Media can be played in segments of definable length, with looping and other options. Soundscriber is free transcription software.

The last program is Writer's Blocks. This software provides applications for writing, saving, printing, and exporting data.

FREE-FORM TEXT DATABASES

Some database programs are designed for free-form text and may be useful for qualitative research. One example of a free-form text program is AskSam for unstructured research. AskSam handles either free-form text, or AskSam is a tool for organizing files from Microsoft Word, WordPerfect, the Web, Adobe Acrobat, email, and other sources. The researcher can type notes, thoughts, comments, and other information into AskSam. AskSam lets the researcher create "forms" for the researcher to set up fields for keywords, categories, subjects, dates, or anything else. These fields can help the researcher better organize and manage the researcher information. AskSam comes with predefined templates, many of which have been designed for researchers.

Once the researcher information is in AskSam, the researcher may search by typing words or phrases, and AskSam will list all the matching documents. With AskSam the researcher can search the full text of the researcher documents, or the researcher can restrict the search to specific fields (perhaps Title, Keywords, or Notes). The researcher can search by date, use wildcard searches, fuzzy searches, and proximity searches. AskSam offers a set of tools to organize and analyze information. Output lists of the researcher documents may be sorted by title, author, or any other fields. Reports give the researcher an overview of the researcher information. The researcher can create hypertext to navigate between the researcher documents, create links that connect bits and pieces of information or provide an overview of the researcher documents and the researcher can link to external documents or websites. The AskSam's show command lets the researcher search the researcher documents and output text fragments containing a word or phrase. For example, the researcher could generate a list of every paragraph from every document containing the phrase "information literacy."

In addition to all of the specialized software programs discussed in this chapter, a researcher can use the programs that are available through the Microsoft suite. Microsoft Word is particularly helpful for word finds in Level 1 coding. Access, Excel, and Outlook are useful for Level 2 coding. Access and Excel may also be used for Levels 3 and 4 coding. Hahn (2008) provides an excellent resource for the appropriate uses of Microsoft Word software and qualitative coding.

SOFTWARE FOR PRESENTING QUALITATIVE DATA

An hour of conversation may be thousands of words. The researcher will need software to help with organizing data in a meaningful and concise format. If the researcher produces a report or gives a written presentation, she or he will need to describe the research process, give the conclusions, and present data to back them up typically in less than an hour. One of the main problems with qualitative research is how to pick out the relatively small amount of data that the researcher can actually use in a presentation. Microsoft Word and Word Perfect have outlining and hyperlink features that are helpful in organizing presentation materials.

Outlining allows the researcher to organize large quantities of text. Outlining also allows the researcher provide an overview of the text in meaningful chunks.

Hyperlinks can be created so that the reader can be taken to another part of the same document or to another document. Hyperlinks are useful for providing definitions, descriptions, and supplemental material.

MULTIMEDIA PRESENTATION

Compiling presentations on CD is one method for assimilating data along with audio and video files. Commonly available tools such an HTML editor, PowerPoint, Quick-Time, and Adobe Acrobat are helpful for report presentations.

If the recipients of the report do not have the necessary software, you can include the software for free players on a CD. You will need to obtain the necessary permissions from all individuals for photos and taped comments.

CASE STUDY MATRICES

Case study researchers typically use matrices and other data displays to analyze full data sets. The researcher might begin with a draft chart containing a metamatrix displaying common elements of several cases. The researcher develops descriptive or conceptual displays, time-order matrices, effects matrices, and composite sequence analysis showing correlations between time, concepts, behaviors, and cause and effect relationships. The cases may later be regrouped for the final analysis to show clusters of cases that show common characteristics. Regrouping cases sometimes provides a different perspective for the researcher and for the stakeholders.

Matrices can be extremely helpful in organizing and displaying data. Miles and Huberman (1994) provide some outstanding examples of matrices that are appropriate for all phases of a case study, including the final report. Most of these matrices can be produced using some of the software packages that have been discussed in this chapter. They also include a chapter on some rules of thumb for drawing conclusions from matrix data. Well-ordered matrices help us to see qualitative data analysis as a whole.

The following list of resources will give other examples and templates for developing matrices.

Alvord, B. *Assessment Clear and Simple: A Practical Guide for Institutions, Departments, and General Education*. San Francisco: Jossey-Bass, 2004.

Brimley, R. *The Academic Library Manager's Forms, Policies, and Procedures Handbook*. New York: Neal-Schuman, 2007.

Creswell, J., & Clark, V. *Designing and Conducting Mixed Methods Research*. Thousand Oaks: Sage, 2007.

Dudden, R. *Using Benchmarking, Needs Assessment, Quality Improvement, Outcome Measurement, and Library Standards*. Medical Library Association Guides. New York: Neal-Schuman, 2004.

Matthews, J. *Library Assessment in Higher Education*. Westport, CT: Libraries Unlimited, 2007.

Miller, B. *Assessing Organizational Performance in Higher Education*. San Francisco: Jossey-Bass, 2007.

Neely, T. *Information Literacy Assessment: Standards-Based Tools and Assignments*. Chicago: ALA, 2006.

REFERENCES

Hahn, C. *Doing Qualitative Research Using Your Computer: A Practical Guide*. Thousand Oaks, CA: Sage, 2008.

Miles, M., & Huberman, A. *Qualitative Data Analysis: An Expanded Sourcebook*, 2nd ed. Thousand Oaks, CA: Sage, 1994.

Weitzman, E., & Miles, M. *Computer Programs for Qualitative Data Analysis: A Software Sourcebook*. Thousand Oaks, CA: Sage, 1995.

WEBLIOGRAPHY OF QUALITATIVE SOFTWARE

AskSam: http//www.AskSam.com/sem/?s=Google_AskSam_Research&kw=Research
ATLAS.ti: http//www.atlasti.de/
BBEdit: http//www.apple.com/downloads/macosx/productivity_tools/bbedit.html
The Ethnograph: http//www.qualisresearch.com/
HyperResearch: http//www.researchware.com/?gclid=CNy2g-yjkIYCFSU6SgodIS6Usw
Nisus: http//www.nisus.com/Products/
NVivo: www.qsrinternational.com
Writer's Block: http//www.writersblocks.com/wb3download.htm

OTHER SOURCES ON QUALITATIVE SOFTWARE

A useful link is CAQDAS (Computer-assisted qualitative data analysis software).

RESOURCES FOR QUALITATIVE RESEARCHERS

Judy Norris's site at the University of Georgia: http//www.qualitativeresearch.uga.edu/QualPage/
Information on qualitative data analysis, software, and references: James Drisko's site, from
      Smith College in the US

Appendix A: *The Program Evaluation Standards*

SUMMARY OF THE STANDARDS

Utility Standards

The utility standards are intended to ensure that an evaluation will serve the information needs of intended users.

U1 Stakeholder Identification Persons involved in or affected by the evaluation should be identified, so that their needs can be addressed.

U2 Evaluator Credibility The persons conducting the evaluation should be both trustworthy and competent to perform the evaluation, so that the evaluation findings achieve maximum credibility and acceptance.

U3 Information Scope and Selection Information collected should be broadly selected to address pertinent questions about the program and be responsive to the needs and interests of clients and other specified stakeholders

U4 Values Identification The perspectives, procedures, and rationale used to interpret the findings should be carefully described, so that the bases for value judgments are clear.

U5 Report Clarity Evaluation reports should clearly describe the program being evaluated, including its context, and the purposes, procedures, and findings of the evaluation, so that essential information is provided and easily understood.

U6 Report Timeliness and Dissemination Significant interim findings and evaluation reports should be disseminated to intended users, so that they can be used in a timely fashion.

U7 Evaluation Impact Evaluations should be planned, conducted, and reported in ways that encourage follow-through by stakeholders, so that the likelihood that the evaluation will be used is increased.

Feasibility Standards

The feasibility standards are intended to ensure that an evaluation will be realistic, prudent, diplomatic, and frugal.

F1 Practical Procedures The evaluation procedures should be practical, to keep disruption to a minimum while needed information is obtained.

F2 Political Viability The evaluation should be planned and conducted with anticipation of the different positions of various interest groups, so that their cooperation may be obtained, and so that possible attempts by any of these groups to curtail evaluation operations or to bias or misapply the results can be averted or counteracted.

F3 Cost Effectiveness The evaluation should be efficient and produce information of sufficient value, so that the resources expended can be justified

Propriety Standards

The propriety standards are intended to ensure that an evaluation will be conducted legally, ethically, and with due regard for the welfare of those involved in the evaluation, as well as those affected by its results.

P1 Service Orientation Evaluations should be designed to assist organizations to address and effectively serve the needs of the full range of targeted participants.

P2 Formal Agreements Obligations of the formal parties to an evaluation (what is to be done, how, by whom, when) should be agreed to in writing, so that these parties are obligated to adhere to all conditions of the agreement or formally to renegotiate it.

P3 Rights of Human Subjects Evaluations should be designed and conducted to respect and protect the rights and welfare of human subjects.

P4 Human Interactions Evaluators should respect human dignity and worth in their interactions with other persons associated with an evaluation, so that participants are not threatened or harmed.

P5 Complete and Fair Assessment The evaluation should be complete and fair in its examination and recording of strengths and weaknesses of the program being evaluated, so that strengths can be built upon and problem areas addressed.

P6 Disclosure of Findings The formal parties to an evaluation should ensure that the full set of evaluation findings along with pertinent limitations are made accessible to the persons affected by the evaluation and any others with expressed legal rights to receive the results.

P7 Conflict of Interest Conflict of interest should be dealt with openly and honestly, so that it does not compromise the evaluation processes and results.

P8 Fiscal Responsibility The evaluator's allocation and expenditure of resources should reflect sound accountability procedures and otherwise be prudent and ethically responsible, so that expenditures are accounted for and appropriate

Accuracy Standards

The accuracy standards are intended to ensure that an evaluation will reveal and convey technically adequate information about the features that determine worth or merit of the program being evaluated.

A1 Program Documentation The program being evaluated should be described and documented clearly and accurately, so that the program is clearly identified.

A2 Context Analysis The context in which the program exists should be examined in enough detail, so that its likely influences on the program can be identified.

A3 Described Purposes and Procedures The purposes and procedures of the evaluation should be monitored and described in enough detail, so that they can be identified and assessed.

A4 Defensible Information Sources The sources of information used in a program evaluation should be described in enough detail, so that the adequacy of the information can be assessed.

A5 Valid Information The information-gathering procedures should be chosen or developed and then implemented so that they will assure that the interpretation arrived at is valid for the intended use.

A6 Reliable Information The information-gathering procedures should be chosen or developed and then implemented so that they will assure that the information obtained is sufficiently reliable for the intended use.

A7 Systematic Information The information collected, processed, and reported in an evaluation should be systematically reviewed, and any errors found should be corrected.

A8 Analysis of Quantitative Information Quantitative information in an evaluation should be appropriately and systematically analyzed so that evaluation questions are effectively answered.

A9 Analysis of Qualitative Information Qualitative information in an evaluation should be appropriately and systematically analyzed so that evaluation questions are effectively answered.

A10 Justified Conclusions The conclusions reached in an evaluation should be explicitly justified, so that stakeholders can assess them.

A11 Impartial Reporting Reporting procedures should guard against distortion caused by personal feelings and biases of any party to the evaluation, so that evaluation reports fairly reflect the evaluation findings.

A12 Metaevaluation The evaluation itself should be formatively and summatively evaluated against these and other pertinent standards, so that its conduct is appropriately guided and, on completion, stakeholders can closely examine its strengths and weaknesses.

CITING THE STANDARDS

This page conveys permission for you to include copies of the standards statement in your document or Web site with appropriate reference to the publications.

Generally, all people are allowed to publish and use the standard statements. We ask that the complete reference to the published document be provided, and we encourage reference to the Western Michigan University Web site as well.

The Joint Committee on Standards for Educational Evaluation, Inc. has produced three sets of standards. Standards for Evaluations of Educational Programs, Projects, and Materials was published in 1981, revised (as *The Program Evaluation Standards*) in 1994, and is currently in its 2nd revision. The Personnel Evaluation Standards was published in 1981 and is currently being revised. The Student Evaluation Standards was published in 2003.

http://www.wmich.edu/evalctr/jc/

Appendix B: The Joint Committee on Standards for Educational Evaluation

This document was prepared by the Joint Committee on Standards for Educational Evaluation as a derivative of *The Program Evaluation Standards* (Thousand Oaks, CA: Sage Publications, Inc., 1994). It is a compilation of advice from hundreds of practitioners in education and evaluation regarding one function in the program evaluation process. Other derivative documents related to evaluation functions are available. The evaluation functions covered in this series are

1. Deciding Whether to Evaluate
2. Defining the Evaluation Problem
3. Designing the Evaluation
4. Collecting Information
5. Analyzing Information
6. Reporting the Evaluation
7. Budgeting the Evaluation
8. Contracting for Evaluation
9. Managing the Evaluation
10. Staffing the Evaluation

Stakeholder Identification

1. Identify persons in leadership roles and ask them to identify other stakeholders in the evaluation. Contact representatives of identified stakeholder groups to learn how they view the evaluation's importance, how they would like to use its results, and what particular information

would be useful. Where necessary, help them to develop realistic expectations that take into account the methodological, financial, and political constraints on the evaluation. (U1)

2. Use stakeholders to identify and contact other stakeholders (U1)
3. Reach an understanding with the client concerning the relative importance of the potential stakeholders and the information they desire, and plan and implement the data collection and the reporting activities accordingly (U1)
4. Throughout the evaluation, be alert to identifying additional stakeholders that should be served and, within the limits of time and resources, maintain some flexibility and capability to respond to their needs (U1)
5. Involve clients and other stakeholders directly in designing and conducting the evaluation (U1)
6. Be certain not to exclude any stakeholder because of gender, ethnicity, or language background (U1)
7. Do not allow clients to inappropriately restrict the evaluator's contact with other involved or affected stakeholders (U1)
8. Do not attempt to address all stakeholder information needs when, in reality, they cannot all be addressed (U1)
9. Do not assume that persons in leadership or decision making roles are the only, or most important, stakeholders (U1)
10. Avoid over identifying stakeholders making it impossible to proceed (U1)
11. Do not fail to distinguish between the client and other stakeholders (U1)

Evaluator Credibility

12. Stay abreast of social and political forces associated with the evaluation, especially those linked to race, gender, socioeconomic status, and language and cultural differences, and use this knowledge when designing and conducting the evaluation (U2)
13. Ensure that both the work plan and the composition of the evaluation team are responsive to the concerns of key stakeholders (U2)
14. Consider having the evaluation plan reviewed and the evaluation work audited by another evaluator whose credentials are acceptable to the client (U2)
15. Be clear in describing the evaluation plan to various stakeholders and demonstrate that the plan is realistic and technically sound (U2)
16. Determine key audience needs for information on the progress of the evaluation and keep them informed about the progress of the evaluation through such means as newsletters, progress reports, telephone calls, memoranda, press releases, and meetings (U2)
17. Include in evaluation proposals a statement describing the evaluator's qualifications relevant to the program being evaluated (U2)
18. Seek evaluators experienced in the setting of the evaluation (U2)
19. Do not over invest resources to achieve credibility and acceptance (U2)
20. Do not assume that the evaluator's approach to evaluation is acceptable to the client (U2)
21. Avoid turning over the evaluation to an inexperienced student or staff assistant (U2)

Information Scope and Selection

22. Understand client requirements for the evaluation (U3)
23. Interview representatives of major stakeholders to gain an understanding of their different and perhaps conflicting points of view and of their need for information (U3)

24. Avoid giving the impression that all questions will be answered (U3)
25. Help stakeholders develop realistic expectations in light of available financial, time, and personnel resources (U3)
26. Have the client rank potential audiences in order of importance and work with representatives of each stakeholder group to rank topics in order of importance to that audience (U3)
27. Work with the client to collate the ordered topics from each audience, to remove items at the bottom of the list, and to add items that the evaluator believes to be important even though not requested (U3)
28. Allow flexibility for adding questions and including unanticipated information that may arise during the evaluation (U3)
29. Distribute the entire evaluation effort (data collection, analysis, interpretation, and reporting) over the final list of topics, placing the most effort on high-ranked items (U3)
30. Consider the tradeoffs between comprehensiveness and selectivity at every stage of the evaluation developing the plan; setting the budget; and collecting, analyzing, interpreting, and reporting information (U3)
31. Give voice to multiple stakeholder groups in the process of selecting priority evaluation questions (U3)
32. Do not collect information because it is convenient (e.g., because instruments already exist), rather than because it is necessary (U3)
33. Delimit the scope of the evaluation, i.e., failing to state the questions that will be answered and the purpose of the evaluation, and keeping them in mind at every stage of the evaluation (U3)
34. Do not collect information that is extraneous to the central purpose of the evaluation (U3)

Values Identification

35. Consider alternative bases for interpreting findings e.g., program objectives, procedural specifications, laws and regulations, institutional goals, democratic ideals, social norms, performance by a comparison group, assessed needs of a consumer group, expected performance of the sample group, professional standards, and reported judgments by various reference groups (U4)
36. Consider who will make interpretations e.g., the evaluators, the client, the various stakeholders, a regulatory group, or some combination of these (U4)
37. Consider alternative techniques that might be used to assign value meanings to collected information e.g., having different teams write advocacy reports; conducting a jury or administrative trial of the program being evaluated; or seeking convergence through a Delphi study (U4)
38. Do not assume that evaluations can be objective in the sense of being devoid of value judgment (U4)
39. Do not design the data collection and analysis procedures without considering what criteria, such as performance by a comparison group or performance in terms of a predetermined standard, will be needed to interpret the findings (U4)
40. Do not concentrate so heavily on clarifying values that insufficient time and effort are devoted to collecting and analyzing the information needed to make value judgments (U4)
41. Acknowledge that decision rules often are arbitrary and therefore subject to debate (U4)

Practical Procedures

42. Ensure the availability of qualified personnel to complete the evaluation as proposed, including the need to train any personnel who need it (F1)

43. Choose procedures that can be carried out with reasonable effort and that are compatible with the skill level of personnel available for the study (F1)
44. Select procedures in light of known time constraints and the availability of participants or respondents (F1)
45. Whenever appropriate, make evaluation activities a part of routine events (F1)
46. Develop alternative procedures in anticipation of potential problems and retain sufficient flexibility in the plan and budget so that unanticipated problems can be addressed as they occur (F1)
47. Check with the clients about the viability of the schedule for completing the evaluation and the practicality of various data collection procedures before finalizing the data collection plan (F1)
48. Try out procedures and instruments in a pilot test to determine their practicality and their time requirements (F1)
49. Avoid choosing a data collection and analysis plan from a research methods textbook or other general guide without considering whether the plan can be carried out in the given setting (F1)
50. Do not fail to weigh practicality against accuracy—if circumstances will inhibit the collection of valid and reliable data, work with the client to remove or alter these circumstances. If this proves unsuccessful, seriously consider using other procedures or not doing the evaluation. (F1)
51. Avoid disrupting program activities in an attempt to collect information (F1)

Formal Agreements

52. Include the evaluation design in any formal agreements (P2)
53. Do not expect participation in the evaluation by persons who have not previously agreed to do so (P2)
54. Do not act unilaterally in a matter where it has been agreed that evaluator/client collaboration would be required for decisions (P2)
55. Do not change the design without amending formal agreements (P2)
56. Do not adhere so rigidly to contracts that changes dictated by common sense are not made or are unduly delayed (P2)
57. Do not develop contracts that are so detailed that they stifle the creativity of the evaluation team or that detract from conducting the evaluation (P2)

Complete and Fair Assessments

58. Design the evaluation to record both strengths and weaknesses of the program being evaluated (P5)

Program Documentation

59. Ask the client and the other stakeholders to describe—orally and, if possible, in writing—the intended and the actual program with reference to such characteristics as personnel, cost, procedures, location, facilities, setting, activities, objectives, nature of participation, and potential side effects (A1)
60. Collect and analyze for differences and similarities available descriptions of the program, including proposals, public relations reports, slide-tape presentations, and staff progress and final reports (A1)
61. Engage independent observers to describe the program if time and budget permit (A1)
62. Set aside time at the beginning of the evaluation to observe the program and the staff and participants who are involved (A1)

63. As part of the ongoing evaluation process, maintain up-to-date descriptions of the program from different information sources (e.g., participant observers, minutes of staff meetings, interviews of participants, and progress reports), giving particular attention to changes in the description (A1)
64. Consider developing separate descriptions for each aspect of the program being studied (A1)
65. Do not rely solely on the client's or the funding proposal's description of the program (A1)
66. Do not gloss over a description of the program by saying, for example, that "the treatment was all that occurred between time 1 and 2," without describing the actual events (A1)
67. Do not concentrate so much on describing the program that insufficient time is available for assessing its strengths and weaknesses (A1)
68. Do not assume that the program is uniformly implemented as intended (A1)

Described Purposes and Procedures

69. Discuss thoroughly and record the client's initial conceptions of the purposes of the evaluation, and the intended uses of the findings from the evaluation (A3)
70. Discuss thoroughly and record the client's initial conceptions of how the evaluation's purposes will be achieved (A3)
71. Keep a copy of the evaluation plan and the evaluation contract (if one was negotiated) (A3)
72. Reach a clear understanding with the client of major changes in evaluation purposes and procedures as the changes are made (A3)
73. Record any major changes in purposes and procedures and the date on which they occurred (A3)
74. Plan to describe purposes and procedures at the conclusion of the evaluation in both a summary report (executive report) and a full technical report, noting deviations from original plans (A3)
75. Engage independent evaluators to monitor the purposes and procedures of the evaluation, and evaluate them whenever feasible, especially in the case of large-scale evaluations (A3, A12)
76. Allow for the adjustments in purpose and procedure that may be needed during the evaluation (A3)

Described Information Sources

77. Use previously collected information that is pertinent to the evaluation once its soundness has been determined (A4)
78. Do not assume that information based on personal interviews, testimony, observations, or document analysis contains distortions, and hence is not worthy of consideration. Conversely, assuming that "hard" quantitative data lack distortion and hence should be weighted heavily in evaluation. (A4)
79. For each data collection activity describe and justify the sources of information to be used in the study (A4)
80. Assess the adequacy of the information sources as part of the technical documentation of the evaluation, acknowledging limitations that may exist (A4)

Valid Information

81. Check information collection procedures against the objectives and content of the program being evaluated to determine the degree of fit or congruence between them. This check should be informed at least in part by personnel responsible for the program and its operation and by representatives of important stakeholder groups. (A5)

82. Consider the *Standards for Educational and Psychological Testing* and other available sets of standards, and apply them when making decisions about educational and psychological tests to be used in the evaluation (A5)

83. Consider validity evidence from other similar evaluations in which proposed procedures were used (A5)

84. Ensure that the individuals who will administer or use a particular procedure are qualified and adequately prepared (in terms of knowledge, training, and practice) to do so (A5)

85. For newly developed procedures, present the rationale for the extent of validity claimed. Point out that such procedures are exploratory, and that results obtained from them must be interpreted cautiously and with a clear understanding of the limited validity evidence. Further, proper account must be taken of the context, the characteristics of the subjects or groups with whom the procedure was used, and the qualifications and training, if needed, of the individuals who administered or used the procedure. Use multiple measures to help clarify the validity of the inferences drawn from the information yielded by the new procedure. (A5)

86. Use multiple procedures to obtain a more comprehensive assessment, but do so in as nondisruptive and parsimonious a manner as possible. Often it is desirable to employ nonreactive procedures, and to assess samples instead of populations of respondents. Use existing records, if relevant. (A5)

87. Assess the comprehensiveness of the information provided by the procedures as a set in relation to the information needed to answer the set of evaluation questions (A5)

88. Consider respondent characteristics, such as reading ability, language proficiency, or physical handicaps, that may affect the validity of evaluation results (A5)

89. Do not base important decisions on only one procedure or operational definition of a critical variable (A5)

90. Do not expect that procedures yielding valid inferences can be constructed or developed quickly and easily (A5)

91. Use existing procedures yielding valid inferences when they are available (A5)

92. Ensure that personnel responsible for collecting information are adequately qualified and prepared to perform their assigned tasks (A5)

93. Ensure that observations and descriptions of a process or event are adequately conducted and completed (A5)

94. Allow qualified stakeholders the opportunity to review an instrument or procedure prior to its use (A5)

Reliable Information

95. Whenever possible, evaluators should choose information gathering procedures that have, in the past, yielded data and information with acceptable reliability for their intended uses; however, the generalizability of previously favorable reliability results may not be simply assumed. Reliability information should be collected that is directly relevant to the group and ways in which the information gathering procedures will be used in the evaluation. (A6)

96. For newly developed information gathering procedures, present the rationale for the type and extent of reliability claimed. Proper account must be taken of the content or behavior assessed by the procedure, of the ways in which the procedures were administered to the subjects or groups, and of the heterogeneity of the persons in terms of the characteristics being measured or observed, for these factors all influence reliability. (A6)

97. Discuss developing propositions, interpretations, and conclusions with an impartial peer to help clarify own posture and values and their role in the inquiry (A6)

98. In the case of open ended instruments and procedures, check the consistency of scoring, categorization, and coding by two or more qualified persons independently analyzing the same set of information or by an outside auditor verifying that the data have been consistently analyzed (A6)

99. Provide adequate training to scorers and analysts to ensure that they are sensitized to the kinds of mistakes they are likely to make, and know the procedures to avoid these mistakes (A6)

100. Do not interpret evidence of one type of reliability (e.g., internal consistency, stability over time, interobserver agreement) as evidence of another type, i.e., different reliabilities reflect different sources of measurement error which influence the interpreting of information in different ways (A6)

101. Do not rely upon the reliability evidence that is reported for a published instrument or procedure taken at face value without considering the likely effects of differences between the setting and sample of the reported reliability study and those of the evaluation (A6)

102. Take into account the fact that the reliability of the scores provided by an instrument or procedure may fluctuate depending on how, when, and to whom the instrument or procedure is administered (A6)

103. Do not assume that because the reliability of individual scores for an instrument is low, the reliability of mean scores for a group will also be low (A6)

104. Do not interpret reliability coefficients for measures of continuous variables as evidence of the reliability of dichotomous decisions (eg., pass-fail; mastery-nonmastery) based on these measures (A6)

105. Recognize that the reliability of a set of difference scores is typically less than the reliability of either of the two sets of scores used to compute the differences (A6)

106. Do not use scores with low reliabilities as influential outcome information (A6)

107. Do not assume that because reliability is high, validity is also high (A6)

108. Do not assume that the observations of one evaluator are not affected by the evaluator's perspective, training, or previous experience (A6)

Analysis of Quantitative Information

109. Choose analytic procedures that are appropriate to the evaluation questions and the nature of the data (A8)

110. Conduct multiple analyses of the data, as is usually warranted (A8)

111. Report potential weaknesses in the study design or data analysis and describe their possible influence on interpretations and conclusions (e.g., attrition, violation of assumptions) (A8)

112. Do not assume that significant statistical results are necessarily of practical significance (A8)

113. Do not assume that gain scores, matching, or analysis of covariance will necessarily provide an adequate adjustment for preexisting differences among groups (A8)

114. Use the correct unit of analysis when analyzing quantitative information (U8)

115. Do not use complex statistical techniques when the audience would be better served by the use of simpler analytical methods and graphs (A8)

116. Avoid emphasizing rigor at the expense of relevance, and vice versa (A8)

117. All evaluations do not need to use statistical analyses (A8)

118. All evaluations do not need to be comparative studies (A8)

119. Recognize and exploit the complementarity between qualitative and quantitative analyses and that interpretations and conclusions should be supported by both (A8)

Analysis of Qualitative Information

120. Choose an analytic procedure and method of summarization that is appropriate to the questions to be addressed in the study and to the nature of the qualitative information to be collected (A9)
121. Focus the analysis on clear questions of interest and define the boundaries of information to be examined, e.g., time period, funded activities, target student or other client population, and geographic location (A9)
122. Seek corroboration of qualitative evidence using independent methods and sources (A9)
123. Do not regard qualitative data analysis as relatively nonrigorous and as something that can be accomplished well enough on an intuitive basis without training, choosing information to reinforce preconceptions rather than examine the validity of preconceptions or working hypotheses (A9)
124. Consider alternative interpretations of reality and the multiple value perspectives that may exist in an evaluation situation (A9)
125. Distinguish among different sources of qualitative information on such bases as credibility, degree of expertise, and degree of involvement (A9)

Justified Conclusions

126. Plan to generate, assess, and report plausible alternative explanations of the findings, and, where possible, indicate why these explanations should be discounted (A10)
127. Plan to solicit feedback from a variety of program participants about the credibility of interpretations, explanations, conclusions, and recommendations before finalizing reports. Plan to point out common misinterpretations and inappropriate inferences that may be drawn from the information collected (A10)
128. Attend to possible side effects of the program in reaching conclusions about its effectiveness (A10)

Impartial Reporting

129. Reach agreement with the client during the initial stages of the evaluation about the steps to be taken to ensure the fairness of all reports (A11)
130. Clarify the nature of and authority for editing (A11)
131. Ensure the evaluation report includes perspectives independent of the perspectives of those whose work is being evaluated (A11)
132. Plan to seek out and report alternative, perhaps even conflicting, conclusions and recommendations (A11)
133. Strive to establish and maintain independence in reporting, using techniques such as adversary-advocacy reports, outside audits, or rotation of evaluation team members over various audience contacts (A11)
134. Do not assume that all parties in an evaluation are neutral (A11)
135. Avoid surrendering the authority to edit reports (A11)
136. Be involved in public presentations of the findings as the situation warrants (A11)
137. Do not become so isolated from the program developer that potentially useful information from the developer is not reported to the evaluator, and there is no good way for feedback to be transmitted from the evaluator to the program developer (A11)

Metaevaluation

138. Budget sufficient money and other resources to conduct appropriate formative and summative metaevaluations (A12)

139. Assign someone responsibility for documenting and assessing the program evaluation process and products (A12)

140. Consider asking a respected professional body to nominate someone to chair a team of external metaevaluators in large evaluations. Failing that, either (a) appoint a team and have it elect the chair, or (b) carefully and judiciously select as chair someone who will be competent and credible, and work with this individual to appoint other team members. (A12)

141. Determine and record the rules by which members of the metaevaluation team will reach a consensus and/or issue minority reports (A12)

142. Stipulate that any member of the metaevaluation team who does not fulfill contracted obligations can be dismissed at the discretion of the chair (A12)

143. Reserve final authority for editing the metaevaluation report to the metaevaluators (A12)

144. Determine and record which audiences will receive the metaevaluation reports and how the reports will be transmitted (A12)

145. Evaluate the instrumentation, data collection, data handling, coding, and analysis of the program evaluation to determine how carefully and effectively these steps were implemented (A12)

146. Expect that the metaevaluation itself will be subject to rebuttal and evaluation, and maintain a record of all metaevaluation steps, information, and analyses (A12)

147. Do not conduct only an internal metaevaluation when conflict of interest or other considerations clearly establish the need for an external metaevaluation (A12)

148. Do not assume that every program evaluation study requires a formal metaevaluation study (A12)

Partial support for the development of these derivative documents came from the National Science Foundation under award number SED-9255369 to Westat, Inc. The Joint Committee takes full responsibility for its content. Generally, all people are allowed to publish and use the standard statements. We ask that the complete reference to the published document be provided, and we encourage reference to the Western Michigan University Web site as well. The Joint Committee on Standards for Educational Evaluation, Inc. has produced three sets of standards. *Standards for Evaluations of Educational Programs, Projects, and Materials* was published in 1981, revised (as *The Program Evaluation Standards*) in 1994, and is currently in its 2nd revision. *The Personnel Evaluation Standards* was published in 1981 and is currently being revised. *The Student Evaluation Standards* was published in 2003.

Index

About the Author

RAVONNE A. GREEN, PhD, is the author of *Library Management: A Case Study Approach* (2007) and coauthor of *Keep It Simple: A Guide to Assistive Technologies* (Libraries Unlimited 2011, with Vera Blair).

CPSIA information can be obtained at www.ICGtesting.com
Printed in the USA
LVOW09s2229240715

447487LV00010B/27/P